THE SUCCESSFUL TEACHING SERIES

TEENS: GIVING YOUTH THE GROW-AHEAD

LAWRENCE O. RICHARDS, PH.D.

David C. Cook Publishing Co.
ELGIN, ILLINOIS/WESTON, ONTARIO

Note: The first edition of this book appeared under the title, *You and Youth*.

© 1988 David C. Cook Publishing Co.

Scripture quotations, unless otherwise noted, are from the *Holy Bible: New International Version*, © 1973, 1978, 1984 by the New York International Bible Society, used by permission of Zondervan Bible Publishers.

Published by David C. Cook Publishing Co.
850 N. Grove Ave., Elgin, IL 60120
Cable address: DCCOOK

Designer: Dawn Lauck
Cover illustration: Bob Fuller
Printed in U.S.A.
Library of Congress Catalog Card Number: 87-63568
ISBN:1-55513-167-0

CONTENTS

ABOUT THIS BOOK

This is a specialized book. It's for teachers whose ministry is specifically with young people. And it's part of a series—the Successful Teaching Series. Its distinctive focus makes it an excellent companion to the first book in the series, *Teaching with Love,* which covers the basics for all teachers.

You may want to look at this book, then, as an "advanced course" for a person who specializes. But even though you may be a specialist, you can't afford to overlook the basics! If reading and studying this book raise any questions about who you are as a teacher of God's Word, or how you can best perform this basic ministry, you'll want to study the first and foundational book.

One other note. This is a *study* book, designed to help you grow in your ministry. You'll find that your growth is stimulated if you take the time to work through the suggestions following each chapter. Just as the key to the growth of your young people is in how they respond to what you teach, the key to your growth as a teacher is in how you respond and use ideas and suggestions you find in this book or other sources.

Young people are special. It's challenging and exciting to work with them and see God shaping their lives. It's a ministry that has eternal rewards for you— and for your youth. Let's minister wisely—and well.

CHAPTER ONE
COME ALONG

▶High school Sunday School classes across the country take various, typical shapes. I've seen these shapes reproduced over and over in the Midwest, on the East and West coasts, and in the Southwest, too. I want to visit three of them now.

So come along. Perhaps you'll see your class portrayed in this first chapter. Perhaps not. But certainly you'll see some of the problems that crop up as we seek to teach God's Word to young people. And as you read on in this book, you'll find principles that show us how to solve them.

Class One
It's cold outside. As the kids come into the high school classroom, their cheeks are still glowing, and they're rubbing their hands as they chat with each other. Some of them sit down right away, but most cluster in little groups toward the back of the five rows of chairs set up for the 30 or so who usually show up Sunday mornings. Mr. Carlson, the teacher, is standing near the front of the room, glancing at his watch, waiting.

7

GIVING YOUTH THE GROW-AHEAD

Finally it's 9:30, and even though only about half the kids are there—you can hear the others outside in the hall, talking and laughing—Mr. Carlson calls Sue and asks her to play the piano so they can get started. (Marilyn, the regular pianist, hasn't shown up yet, and Mr. C is understandably annoyed. This isn't the first time Marilyn's shown her irresponsibility.)

Mark, one of the senior guys, leads the singing. It's halfhearted, and as other kids straggle in, it's disrupted. Two or three kids have to make announcements: the youth meeting that evening, a social coming up soon, getting in reservations for the semester-break retreat. After another song, Mr. Carlson gets up and begins the morning lesson. It's 9:55.

Mr. Carlson is obviously well prepared. He's teaching a series about distinctive Bible doctrines. ("Something the kids really need before they go off to college," is the way he puts it.) He's working from an outline that has been carefully thought through, and he illustrates nearly every point with a quote from some well-known Bible teacher or commentary. Just listening to him, you can pick up his outline easily.

Salvation
   I. How we know people need salvation
      A. We can see sin's effects all around us (cf. Rom. 1:18-24).
      B. We can feel sin's impact within us.
      C. We know what God has revealed about people's need (Rom. 3:23).
   II. How salvation has been provided
      A. God's love was His motivation for providing salvation (Jn. 3:16).
      B. God's Son died on the cross to pay for salvation (Rom. 5:8).

8

C. God saves all who by faith receive His Son as
   Savior (Jn. 1:12).
III. What salvation means to us
   A. We receive forgiveness for past sin (Rom. 3:25,
      26).
   B. We are free from present sin (Rom. 6:4).
   C. There will be future removal of our sin nature
      (Rom. 8:29, 30).
IV. Questions we may have about salvation
   A. Are we sure we *are* saved? How can we know?
   B. Can salvation be lost?
   C. Are non-Christians really lost? What about our
      responsibility to them?

There's so much material that it's easy to see why Mr.
Carlson hurries on—not that he doesn't try to involve
the teens. He asks kids to look up verses and read
them. He asks them to explain what the verses mean.
He even pauses every now and then to ask, "Do you
have any questions? Is everything clear?"

But for all his preparation and study, for all his
concern that the teens understand important Bible
doctrines, for all his taking time for questions, it's clear
that Mr. Carlson just isn't communicating. There are
many signs: the kids in the back are whispering and
passing notes to each other; the kids up front are just
sitting there, trying to look attentive, but really just
looking blank; there aren't any volunteers when
questions are asked. Mr. Carlson has to mention a
name ("Tim, what do you think?") before he gets an
answer. Even then the answers are short, factual, and
given without elaboration. Sure, most of the kids seem
to know the answers, but no one is very excited about
them. And the teens aren't asking questions on their
own.

Finally, when the bell rings, indicating five minutes to go, the kids begin rustling Bibles, picking up purses, and glancing around the room, obviously eager for release from the room they've occupied for the past hour.

After class is over, Mr. Carlson—a good, solid, concerned teacher who works hard in preparation and wants his kids to get important Bible truths—leaves the classroom, too. He's a little dissatisfied, yet thankful that he's had another opportunity to present the Word to youths who need its instruction.

Class Two

Rod Wedder is a high school teacher. The Sunday School superintendent was delighted when Rod said he'd teach the older teens.

When a person enters Rod's Sunday School room (the class meets in the kitchen), he or she gets an impression of warmth and closeness. The room is smaller than Mr. Carlson's, and more intimate. The chairs are arranged in a circle, so everyone can see and listen more easily. Instead of the 37 teens Mr. Carlson has to deal with, Rod has only 11. And instead of standing up in front, Rod sits right down there in the circle with them. This situation looks—and feels—very different. And you expect a very different kind of class.

The hour starts differently. Instead of a formal opening with singing and announcements, the kids come directly to the kitchen when they arrive at church. Rod is there before the first one comes, and latecomers find the whole gang sitting together in the circle, talking about campus events and whatever's hot on the local scene.

Then class starts, and there's a clear break in the chatter. Mr. Wedder passes out modern language New

Testaments to each of the kids, asks one of them to lead in prayer, and has everyone turn to the Book of Acts. Mr. Wedder feels very strongly that young people need to "know the Bible," so his method of teaching is designed to work through the Scriptures book by book.

"Last week we finished up at Acts 5:14. So let's turn there now and get started. Jim, how about you reading the next paragraph? That's Acts 5:15, 16."

As a result, people brought the sick into the streets and laid them on beds and mats so that at least Peter's shadow might fall on some of them as he passed by. Crowds gathered also from the towns around Jerusalem, bringing their sick and those tormented by evil spirits, and all of them were healed.

When Jim finishes reading, Mr. Wedder starts asking questions.

"Does this remind you of any other incidents or time in the New Testament?"

"How did different groups of people respond to the miracles that Jesus performed?"

"How do you explain the way the average person responded to these apostolic miracles?"

"Do you think that we ought to see miracles in the church today? Would it help in our evangelization?"

Somehow, though the questions are well thought out and probing, the kids in Mr. Wedder's class don't seem too excited about responding. Several times there are long silences, and then Mr. Wedder asks one of the fellows or girls by name. It doesn't seem that the questions are too hard for the kids; they come up with good answers and have some pretty solid thinking to back up their answers when Mr. Wedder asks (as he usually does), "Why do you think that?"

11

GIVING YOUTH THE GROW-AHEAD

When the last question of Acts 5:15, 16 doesn't seem to evoke much interest or debate, Mr. Wedder asks the teen next to Jim to read the next paragraph, Acts 5:17-29. And he repeats the question-answer process.

The group does get into one discussion, over the apostle Peter's answer to the governing council, when it ordered the disciples not to preach Jesus anymore. "We must obey God rather than men" seems to one of the teens to justify disobeying parents when they make unreasonable demands. When the argument begins to get heated, Mr. Wedder settles the question by pointing out that Jesus had specifically told the apostles to "be my witnesses" (Acts 1:8), and so they were obeying a direct command.

"Unless you can come up with a direct command to justify disobeying your parents," Mr. Wedder said, "you'd better not get carried away. Now, let's get back to Acts, shall we?"

The first bell rings. (You can only hear it dimly there in the kitchen.) Mr. Wedder hurries to finish up the paragraph they are dealing with. "All right, gang," he says as the last bell sounds, "we'll pick it up here again next week, with Acts 6."

Rod Wedder leaves class with mixed feelings, too. On the one hand he is satisfied that his kids are getting a good knowledge of the passages they study. But he is disturbed that all his questioning failed to spark the kind of interest and discussion he'd hoped for. But then, it was probably just natural that his teenagers, who talked so animatedly with him about the campus scene, weren't as interested in the Bible as in their daily lives.

But someday they'd be glad they'd gotten to know the Bible thoroughly, as they were learning it now. Someday these studies would do them a lot of good.

Class Three

Carla is a young teacher, the youngest in the
department. And she looks even younger than her 27
years—almost like one of the girls. Looking at her in
the hall, laughing with the kids in her class, matching
them style for style, it is easy to mistake her for one of
the popular teens who flock around her.

In this church, the teens meet with the adults for a
ten-minute opening service. It's clear the kids don't
like it. They move in slowly; and a number of them wait
outside until they hear the song that marks the end of
the opening. And the kids who are inside cluster to the
back and only mouth the words as the superintendent
urges them to sing louder.

When the opening's over, they hurry to their
classrooms.

Carla meets with 14 girls in the pastor's study. She
had only six girls when she took over the class five
months ago; but even the kids who had dropped out
seemed to flow back in, attracted by her outgoing,
vivacious personality. Standing outside the classroom
door, a person can hear a happy hum of voices,
interrupted by laughter; and every now and then it's
quiet, as the conversation grows serious.

Inside all looks busy and happy. The girls lean
forward to hear each other; they look interested and
involved. But there are no Bibles in evidence, except
three under their owners' chairs. Carla talks *with* the
girls, not *to* them (which is usually good). But what
she's saying is puzzling for a Sunday School class.

"What do you want to talk about this week?"

"Well, what did you do when John asked you out,
Jan? Did you tell him how you really felt, or what?"

"I think I probably wouldn't, but I guess that's just
me. What do you think's right?"

"When Ted and I were dating, we used to—"

In some situations most of these teacher's comments would be appropriate—even good. Good teachers will want to know how their teens think and feel about experiences that are important to them. A good teacher won't be overly positive or authoritarian. And a good teacher will share personal incidents with the class. But in Sunday School these things take place *in the context of Bible study.* In Carla's class, the whole time is given to talking, with no attempt made to link the discussion to God's Word, and no effort made to test the girls' thoughts for their harmony with God's revelation. The girls enjoy their time at church with Carla, but they are not led to evaluate their lives by God's standards, or brought closer to Christ through understanding and response to His revelation of Himself in Scripture.

Carla leaves class feeling exhilarated and happy. But her girls leave class with—what?

Inadequate
Probably more than any other word, *inadequate* expresses what's wrong with the three classes we've just visited.

Each class has some things which are good and important, some ingredients that ought to be present in every high school and junior high school Sunday School classroom. But each also lacks other ingredients that are important elements for a *successful* class.

Looking over these three classes again helps us pinpoint some of the elements that are important for successful teaching of youth, and helps us raise questions we need to answer.

What are some of these important areas, and questions they raise? Let's look.

Teacher-student relationship. How is the teacher to

relate to the teens he or she teaches? As a distant authority (Mr. Carlson)? As a friend before class, but firm guide and director in class (Mr. Wedder)? As "one of the gang" (Carla)? What kind of relationship really *facilitates* Bible learning? And how can that relationship be developed between a teacher and his or her class?

Teen involvement. How much should teens be involved in the teaching-learning process, and what makes their participation meaningful? Are teens to be listeners (their role in Mr. Carlson's class)? Are they to think with the teacher about the meaning of the Biblical text (the task Mr. Wedder assigned them)? Are they to share only their personal lives and experiences (apparently Carla's main interest)? Participation is important, but what kind makes Bible study most meaningful? And, how can a teacher get teens to participate on a meaningful level?

Teen motivation. What makes teens *want* to study the Bible? Do we have to just "talk about whatever you want" to get their interest? What motivates young people today, anyway? How can we plug into their concerns and interests, and lead them into Bible study? And how can we motivate youth to *do* the Word they hear?

Content. We certainly all agree that the content we want to study with teens is the Bible. After all, Sunday School is a Bible teaching agency. But what in the Bible do we want to focus on? How do we want to organize the content we're to teach? Do we go to strict, logical organization of Biblical information as the best way to teach the Bible (Mr. Carlson again)? Do we just go verse by verse or paragraph by paragraph (Mr. Wedder)? Or do we just rap, and let the Bible fit in wherever (and if!) it may? Certainly the kids didn't respond with enthusiasm to the Bible as it was taught by either of the two men. Why? And how *can* we organize content effectively?

Purpose. This is another important area of concern. What is the underlying purpose of our class? Mr. Carlson wanted his teens to know basic Bible doctrines so they wouldn't be confused when they went away to college. Mr. Wedder also seemed to focus on the future, and to believe it was important for his kids to know the Bible. Carla seemed to think the Sunday School class was just a place for talk and sharing. Somehow all of these views, while they say something important and right, still end up inadequate. We need a sharper concept of our goal—of *why* we meet with teens Sunday mornings to teach and study the Bible.

Other considerations. There are other aspects of the teaching situation that these three classes illustrate, other questions they raise. For instance, what is the best way to use the short hour most of us have for Sunday Bible teaching? What is the best size for a junior high or high school or college Bible class? What's the best way to arrange the room and have the class seated?

All of these questions are important.

So, as you can see, we have a big task in this little book. It's a task that we can say most simply is to provide answers to the big questions on which successful Bible teaching of youth hinge.

In our search for answers, we'll be examining (in Chapters 2-4) young people themselves, with a view to understanding them better, and seeing why their special ways of experiencing and thinking and feeling create a need for special approaches in teaching. And in our search for answers we'll be examining communication, seeing how a teacher works to create a context in which real and vital communication of God's truth can take place—the kind of communication that moves not merely from the pages of Scripture to the mind, but from the pages of Scripture to the heart and to the life.

We'll be looking for the answers *you* need to become an even more successful teacher of youth.

REACT

1. Look through the three class descriptions in this chapter again. Which of the three (if any) is your class most like? In what ways is your class like and unlike each?

2. Write an objective description of what a visitor to your class would see. What does the description you've written tell you about your class and your teaching?

ACT

1. Read over the many questions listed in the last section of this chapter and underline or check any to which you particularly would like answers.

CHAPTER TWO
THE PUSH AND PULL OF CULTURE

▶Looking back on his high school years, a young man named Gene shares something very revealing about youths' experience. "What I really looked for in high school was popularity. Not that all I strived for was to be popular, but I see now that I wanted to be accepted by the other kids, and that this unconsciously motivated a lot of my thoughts and actions."

What Gene is talking about isn't just the desire to be "in." He's talking about the push and pull of culture.

The pressures inside adolescents that unconsciously motivate thoughts and actions are often perceived by teens as a desire for "popularity." Most young people feel an intense need, although it may appear in various ways in their lives and behaviors. Gene even speaks of the need he experienced as a "controlling" one.

As I look back, I really wasn't the "real" person God intended me to be. I was controlled by trying to be accepted by others.

I know being accepted isn't wrong, but I was trying all the wrong ways. I fought with my parents over clothes, hair, and other things that matter little, all because I thought these things would make me popular or accepted by my peers.

Gene isn't unique. Kristin felt much the same way. She says,

When I was in high school, I didn't care so much if I was real, I just wanted to be comfortable and not self-conscious; and the only way I would be comfortable was if I was popular. This was what I worried and thought about.

Kristin's preoccupation with popularity (acceptance) wasn't a positive force in her life. In fact, it was a highway to unhappiness. Here's how she explains it.

The trouble was, as long as I worried about popularity, I couldn't be comfortable; and if I couldn't be comfortable, I couldn't interact with people; and if I couldn't interact with people, I couldn't be popular. Now, if I wasn't popular I worried about it, and so it was a circle that I saw no way out of. Feeling that people didn't like you and that they were secretly laughing to themselves about you when you went by and thinking that they thought what a dork you were made you feel so crummy you couldn't act like anything but a dork.

Kristin felt caught in a trap, a trap she couldn't break out of.

GIVING YOUTH THE GROW-AHEAD

Strikingly, even kids who seem to have achieved popularity feel the same pressures and tensions. Rob was an extrovert—class president, honor student, and athlete. He says of himself, "I was involved in almost every activity that existed, besides taking piano lessons, keeping a paper route, and operating an amateur radio station. I was liked by my teachers (and could get away with murder in class). I really had it all going for me."

He puts his experience graphically in these words:

I remember times of unequaled happiness and carefree abandon; yet underneath the externals, a general feeling of frustration pervaded. I was at a stage where I didn't fit in either as an adult or a child, and I couldn't seem to find my place in life, where I belonged. I was treated as a child, but I was expected to act like an adult. There was nothing I could grasp ahold of and hang onto; instead I was swept along, not knowing who I was or where I belonged. It was a time when I found myself alone and unprepared to cope with totally new situations. Everything had to be learned by trial and error, and usually I learned a lesson when it was too late to do much good. If only I could have known ahead of time what I would go through—if only to reassure me that I wasn't alone in my struggle.

Usually the inside pressures young people feel don't show up on the outside. Particularly they're not visible to adults who know them only casually. Youth, like the rest of us, learn quickly how to put on masks to hide their real feelings. As Rob says, "People exerted tremendous pressure on me to act according to their expectations. Being a preacher's kid, I had developed an uncanny knack for faking others out and appearing as

if I was all that they expected." We can see the same facility in others. How did people view Kristin, who felt so terribly self-conscious and uncomfortable?
Sometimes as a person who was "funny and made them laugh"; at other times, when acting out spurts of extroversion, as a "flirt," who could laugh and chat with the boys in the hall before passing on.

Pressure

I don't want to overdraw the picture of adolescence as a time of pressure and uncertainty. For most teens there are times of fun and release and happiness. But for nearly all, there are pressure times. They feel these times intensely; they may mask with humor or flippancy or withdrawal, but pressure times are a real and major part of growing up in our culture.

Why are there these experiences of pressure? What explains the push and pull of culture, the need to conform and be accepted?

Largely we can understand it through Rob's words. "I was at a stage where I didn't fit in . . . and I couldn't seem to find my place in life."

'My Place in Life'

Psychologists and sociologists generally think of adolescence as a time of "identity crisis." By this they mean that during the teen and college years, young people work through a process of coming to understand themselves as individuals—as persons in their own right, with their own feelings and attitudes and goals and personalities.

In childhood it's not quite the same. "Who am I?" doesn't trouble children. They're identified by and with their parents. They normally accept themselves as their parents see them, and when asked, "Who are you?"

may respond by giving their mother's or father's name. The cute, shy response of the four-year-old, "I'm Mommy's girl," has far more insight than we imagine!

Childhood is also insulated from the kinds of decisions that force a person to act on his or her own. Clothes, friends, books, bedtimes, and menus are all selected by Mom and Dad. An allowance may give an exciting feeling of freedom and independence, but the choice between the red candy and the green is hardly significant enough to jolt children into questions about who they are or the meaning of their lives.

But childhood passes. And adolescents, with growing powers of thought and deepening ability to feel and wonder, become intensely aware that there is a world beyond their families. It is a world in which people think and feel and act differently, in which the values they have seen expressed in the lives of their parents are challenged by other values and life-styles.

Confronted with issues like these, and placed by high school and by peer friendships in positions where really significant choices must be made, young people are forced to look into themselves and ask, *Who am I? How does a person—like the person I am—act, believe, and feel?* Not every teen senses the pressure in his or her high school years. But for most there's a sense of displacement—an uncertainty about "my place in life."

At times like these, the push and pull of culture exercise their obtrusive control over a young person's thoughts and actions. What is the mechanism of control, the means that opens up a personality to the influence of culture's conflicting values?

People.

Kristin thought of her problem as a "desire for popularity." So did Gene. But really it wasn't that at all.

THE PUSH AND PULL OF CULTURE

To understand what Kristin, Gene, and Rob are talking about, we need to understand the role others play in shaping our personalities. It's easy to see that role by speaking of "family resemblance." It's a common concept, one we're all familiar with. "Isn't he like his dad?" is a phrase we often hear. Sometimes the person who says it will be speaking of a physical trait. But often it will be something else—a character trait, a way of holding his head, a way of reacting to others, a calmness or excitability under tension. And most of us feel there is a rightness about the whole thing. A person *should* somehow be like his or her parent. There *should* be a family resemblance.

But why? Why should a person be like his or her parent? Most simply put, it's because we grow like those we are closest to. Traits of character, personality, and values, are communicated in and through relationships. As we identify with our parents—or with others—we tend to accept and express their values and their behaviors. We take on their way of living and their personalities.

Most teenagers probably couldn't explain this process clearly. But they *do sense* it. And when the time comes that youth, aware of different values and behaviors in our pluralistic culture, feel a need to test the values of their childhood, they instinctively seek out identification with and support from others. Driven to test, to discover who they really are as persons in themselves (not merely as carbon copies of their parents), adolescents feel an intense need for acceptance, for support. They want someone to hold onto while they test the values and ideas all around them—someone to be like, until they decide who they really are, until they find their place in life.

Usually this sense of need for others complicates the

problem and the pressure. Most people feel that to be accepted they need to *conform*—to be, or act like, others. This feeling, in fact, provides the force that both leads youth to act and talk and be like other young people and respond to their fads and music, and also the force that leads them to "act"—to appear to be what others expect them to be at any given time.

So really, the way a guy or girl acts in your Sunday School class—quick to give all the "right" answers, polite, and interested—isn't any indication of how he or she behaves when he or she is with the gang! Young people who develop skill in "conning people" may be troubled by their own inconsistencies. But for a time, many will accept taking on the character of the persons they're with as a way of life and a way of testing different beliefs and different values.

As long as we live in a pluralistic society, a culture in which there are conflicting ideas of right and wrong and style of hair and what dating is all about, young people will continue to feel intense pressures to conform and fit into various groups around them. They may call it a drive for popularity. But in reality it will be a deep-seated need to discover who they are, and to have help as they probe to find out what values a "person like me" can hold and live by.

Check Points
An insight into the pressures of youths growing up in our pluralistic society and the need of youths to identify with others as they try to discover themselves as persons, helps us understand many of the patterns we notice in adolescent life.

The importance of other teens. As young people reach out beyond their childhood identification with the family to establish themselves as individuals, it's important for them to "belong" with others. Teens are thrown into daily contact primarily with other teens. They are, in effect, isolated from the adult world. So it's only natural that we should see the development of a "youth culture."

There are many different groups within this youth culture—ranging from conservative groups of youth, who identify strongly with their parents' values and ideas, to radical kids who reject the establishment totally. Yet there is a broad unity, a unity that means youths see themselves as more like other youth than like the older generation. This unity is marked and maintained by numerous items of culture—fads in dress and hair, special terms and slang expressions, the kind of music that's currently popular (and can change so rapidly). "Youth culture," the sense and signs of unity with other youth, is quite consistent across the country. A fad that starts on the West Coast will soon appear on the East. A term you hear in Wisconsin one week will be used by kids in Florida the next. Being a part of this culture, feeling accepted and not "left out," is important to young people. It's a support youths seek as they try to differentiate themselves from Mom and Dad.

This has many implications for ministry with youth, but one to note particularly is this: Teens are likely to pay more attention to what the other teens are saying than to what *you* say. Not always, of course, but as a general rule, the values and attitudes expressed by other teens in their group will have far more impact than whatever an adult teacher may say—particularly if the teacher only sees them in class on Sunday. We can *expect* most kids to think and feel like others in the group or gang they're closest to.

GIVING YOUTH THE GROW-AHEAD

The pressures to "fit in." Often the thoughts and attitudes—even the actions of a teen—won't really be his or her own. That is, they will not be expressions of his or her personality or character. Often they'll simply be a reflection of what the teen has heard or seen in others.

It's important not to misunderstand the nature of such expressions. They're not necessarily hypocritical—not at all. They may be believed at the moment. More importantly, they may be "tests." That is, they may be a point of view or a behavior that the young person is trying out to see if it fits, to see if this way of thinking or acting seems comfortable and right. And it may very well be that before discovering who he or she is, the young person will test many different patterns of thought and behavior, rejecting some and choosing others, to be part of his or her personality—to become part of him or her.

This is what "character" implies—consistency. This consistency displays itself over time and across situations. Character requires the ability to act in harmony with values that are deeply rooted in the personality; it is something that few young people have during their high school years. Instead of mere consistency, *character* is something we need to help them develop!

But we can't help young people develop character merely by insisting that they adopt *our* standards. Character is something that is, at best and essentially, self-chosen. It reflects standards that a person commits to because he or she understands the importance of life and decides, "This is the kind of person I want to become."

Sometimes, responding to the pressure of peers to adopt their thoughts or behavior, teens will drift into a way of life that captures them imperceptibly and unaware. Often drug or alcohol abuse starts this way, with the idea that it's okay to try it "just this once." Yet peer pressure isn't all bad. Teens can have a positive influence on one another, as in the program called SADD (Students Against Drunk Driving), in which teens influence teens. Even for individuals peer pressure can be a positive thing. Sometimes pressure to do wrong will focus a person's awareness that he or she needs to make a choice, and such choices can lead to commitment.

At any rate, a teacher needs to understand something of *why* young people are particularly sensitive to peer pressure, and why they respond as they do. And we teachers need to understand that, in our teaching of the Bible, we must help young people accept responsibility for their choices, that they might bring every thought into captivity to Christ (II Cor. 10:5).

The tendency to conform. While character is being formed, there's usually a tendency to conform to the expectations of others. Many teens confess to being one person at home and a completely different one at school. And often there's admission of being still a third person in church.

So we can't take young people for granted because they know the right answers, or because they're polite and respectful with us. Rob, the pastor's son, was quick to say how easily he could "con" everyone who knew him. He knew what people expected, and he acted that way.

Somehow we need to know our young people in more than a superficial way. We need to let them know we care about them—even as Jesus cares about them— not because they conform to our expectations, but because they are important to God and to us.

GIVING YOUTH THE GROW-AHEAD

Directions

A little insight into the push and pull of culture in a young person's life tells us much about our task as teachers. We can hardly be satisfied with a superficial brushing up against the teens we teach. We need to know them as individuals. We need to know individuals as they really are, as they really feel, if we are to minister to them most effectively.

If we talk to teens about what helps them find themselves as real persons—about what helps them answer that identity-crisis question, "Who am I?"—we get some significant answers. We hear of people who accept them for what they are, and of commitment.

A guy named J.B. expressed it this way: "As I look back, I can see that the real problem was that I didn't have a set of standards or goals that were really mine, that would help me *be* me. Sure, I had standards set by my parents and even some that I'd taken from my peers, but I didn't have any that were really mine, that I was sure I wanted to live by."

J.B.'s life took on meaning, and he began to develop character when he "came to the place of living by Christ's Spirit and making His fruit (love, joy, peace, long-suffering, etc.), my goals. Until then I was never able to be free to be myself."

God used a teenage friend in J.B.'s life, a friend whose own life showed reality. "I saw that I didn't have Christ's love or forgiveness in me, so I decided I'd try to let Christ run my life."

For many teens, the time of transformation comes when they discover that someone can like and accept them for themselves—without pretense or conformity.

All this is exciting for us as teachers of young people. It's exciting because, sensing the pressures that push and pull teens, *we* have the chance to demonstrate by our own friendship the acceptance they need. And *we* have the chance to share with them the meaning of commitment to Christ and His ways, that they might seek to find with us a distinct identity as Christ's men and women.

REACT

1. If identification with the youth culture is important to teens seeking to establish their own identity, how should adults (parents and teachers) react to things like styles and music? What will attacks on such things likely lead to?

2. If it is often a way of adolescent life to try to fit the expectations of the group of people one is presently with, how can we tell what a young person is "really like" or "really feels"? What might an adult do that would help a young person be himself or herself rather than act a part?

3. If young people respond to the thoughts and attitudes of other youths, how important is it in a Bible-teaching situation to have the teens express themselves freely? What does it say about the effectiveness of a class if teens hesitate to express themselves? Or give only the "expected answers," without discussion and exploration?

ACT

1. List the names of the teens in your class whom you feel you know fairly well. What situations do you see them in? How much of their lives are hidden to you? Are you aware of any feelings of unhappiness or confusion, like those expressed by the young people at the beginning of this chapter?

GIVING YOUTH THE GROW-AHEAD

2. List ways that you might come to know your teens better. How might you let them know that you accept them and want to know them as they really are?

CHAPTER THREE
A STRAIN TOWARD INDEPENDENCE

▶"My mother and father are both Christians, and I have always loved them and known they love me very much," writes Darren. "I have learned to accept and respect their divinely given authority over me and never went through a serious period of rebellion. There were times when I felt they were old-fashioned and didn't understand me, but the majority of these feelings ended between ages 16 and 17.

"I have always been very dependent on my parents; and although there are some areas where I want to be different from them, I see many ways in which I am like them and have accepted many of their ideas and values."

It's great for young persons to have Christian parents who love them deeply and communicate love, and who are the sort of people that their children will want to be. But even in the best of homes, the pull of culture and the adolescent's straining toward an independent identity cause conflict and pain—for both parent and child.

Kelly tells about the worst thing she remembers in her high school years: the parent problem.

I'll never forget all the tears and misery. I didn't feel any different, or that I acted any differently. But I'll never forget Mom in tears telling me that she just couldn't understand what had happened to me—that I had always been so good to them and for them. I, on the other hand, was wondering what had happened to them! It seemed that all we did was fight. My jeans were too tight; I wore too much eye makeup; it wasn't right for me to be the only girl riding in the car from church to youth group at someone's house. I could not ride with Rick because he drove too fast—and Rick was the only one I had cared about driving with for four years! And I knew he usually did drive that way, but he never had when I was with him. They wouldn't listen to that!

Little things, perhaps. But constant bickering about them brought plenty of pain!

It's hard, in little wars like these, to take sides. Surely Kelly's parents were concerned about issues she simply wasn't aware of yet. They tried to act, to restrict, in love. But Kelly was moving out into a world where she was gripped by her own need to fit in, to be like her peers and thus accepted by them. Kelly was struggling to establish herself as a person, and strained desperately for the freedom to make the decisions she felt were rightfully hers to make.

Feeling the strain toward independence, a natural

and important element of growth toward maturity, youths are seldom wise or satisfied. Rob, whom we heard from in the last chapter, looks back at confrontations between himself and his parents with real insight:

> *Most of our confrontations were over very trivial issues (it seems now), such as music, dress, and use of the car. Many times when I couldn't have my way, I really became bitter inside, but it never lasted more than an hour or so. My parents always showed their love at times like these, and we soon made up. Even so, I'd always harbored a sense of injustice done to me, that they really hadn't seen my situation.*
>
> *Looking back, I can see that they definitely handed out as much freedom and responsibility as I could handle, but I was never appreciative or satisfied with what I had. I always wanted to go one better.*

Even when a young person is under the strain toward independence, granting him or her complete freedom isn't really helpful.

For one thing, "complete freedom" is a fantasy. We live in a world in which we are all restricted. We're restricted by requirements of our jobs, by the income we have to spend, by the responsibilities we have to meet. Often we're restricted by our own limitations of ability, of creativity, of love. We live in a world where no one can really do whatever he or she wants. We live lives circumscribed by many limits.

So when young people demand "complete freedom," they're asking for the impossible. And if parents pretend to grant it, youths soon find themselves struggling in a world of illusion, more and more bitter because the meaning and freedom they thought they'd find eludes them. Then their bitterness turns back on the parents who refused to accept *their* responsibility to guide and restrain them.

Certainly, then, as we think about the strain toward independence and granting young people enough freedom to become responsible individuals, we can never think that this means granting "independence," or that it means always letting our young "do their thing," whatever that "thing" may be.

Authority

It's important to understand the youth's experience of authority, for it has great implications for our teaching. The better we understand, the better we will be able to communicate an authoritative Word of God in ways that do not block its acceptance. Today, unlike the 60's and early 70's, young people tend to respect authority and authority figures. But they also expect authorities to be fair and sensitive.

Older people tend to view authority as rooted in status or position. A person obeys a police officer because the officer is a representative of "the law." A student is to do what a teacher says because "she's the teacher." Yet this authority that comes from position is an abstract kind of authority, and young people are very critical when a person in an authority position seems to be unfair. The state of Florida, to name one example, has taken this to heart; in a series of courses that all Florida teachers must complete, the school system is trying to equip staff with communications skills so that their "authority" can be exercised effectively.

The older generation still tends to see submission to authority as simple obedience. Youth want to reserve the right to make their own decisions, and want to be persuaded that what authorities say is valid. My wife, who teaches 11th graders in our local high school, finds the most effective way to maintain order is to take a teen out in the hall and talk to him or her directly about problem behaviors. Often the simple question, "That's not very responsible, is it?" brings agreement and the desired change of behavior. My wife has authority, but in using it with teens tries to keep the young people aware of the fact that they are ultimately responsible for their choices and behaviors.

While doing what an authority figure says may be experienced as surrender, choosing to do what both adult and teen recognize as right is self-chosen submission. In this context of mutual respect, authority is seldom viewed as "evil" and an exercise of authority seldom stimulates resentment or defiance.

There is another element of authority that is important to young people. Older adults may think of authority as something that is essentially impersonal: an objective rule, an impartial but uninvolved policeman or judge. In society this is often just the situation. The umpire does not fraternize with the players. The judge doesn't know personally the prisoner at the bar. And in a way this is ideal.

Yet to my wife's students, and to other teens, this context is ineffective. How can they trust a person who isn't involved with them and who doesn't care? How could an impersonal authority give effective directions? No, the best authority is the one who is involved, and who everyone knows really cares. An involved authority who is fair and who shows that he or she is competent will be respected, and (generally) obeyed.

Every generation of young people tends to think of its experiences as unique. And each generation tends to discount the experiences of adults. While adults sometimes feel that young people should uncritically accept adult opinions, the fact is that teens will not. But they *will* listen to and learn from adults who understand and respect youth's perspectives, who care, and who realize that responding to authority is not giving unquestioned obedience, but rather being willing to listen and ready to agree.

A Context of Love
In the first part of this chapter, I tried to show the straining toward independence in individuals that leads to conflict with parental authority, and that this is reproduced in our youth culture today as a questioning and doubting of authority.

I did it because, as we teach youth, we need to understand the pressures on them and the perspectives on life that are distinctively theirs—particularly where these perspectives conflict with those of many adults.

Certainly understanding won't remove the difficulties or the differences. And it shouldn't. For a young person and for his or her family, there are adjustments that have to be made as growth toward maturity is expressed in a desire (and need) for more responsibility and independence. For older and younger generations of Christians, there are tensions that can only be resolved when each accepts and seeks to understand the other, and when we seek together to come closer to God's perception of authority than either of us has come alone!

But perhaps the important question to ask here has to do with our role as teachers. How can we communicate the trustworthiness of God's Word to youth? How can we help them accept it as a sure and certain guide? How can we encourage them to live by it, to "Taste and see that the Lord is good" (Ps. 34:8)?

Looking again into the experience of teens with their parents gives us clues.

Trying to understand. Laurie found the transition hard when her parents did not seem to understand. "I can still feel the frustration of being almost 13 and knowing no one understood the pain I felt. I have always felt things very deeply. I take life very seriously. And yet everyone thought me a little girl—incapable of any true, significant feelings. It amazes me how forgetful adults can be. One thing I know is that I'll never laugh at or take lightly those feelings and changes I was struggling through then."

Just listening to how young people feel about and perceive their lives, showing that you can accept their experiences as important and serious, can be a great help in communicating. When young people are convinced that we "don't understand," we can hardly expect them to feel that our viewpoints are valid!

Sharing ourselves. When Shannon's dad made a decision that affected the rest of the family, Shannon resisted desperately. The whole household was against Dad's choice, but he remained firm. He was the head of the house, and the children were to obey their parents "in the Lord, for this is right." Shannon went along because she had to, but she was angry and rebellious. As she puts it, "I was only able to see my side of the story and how things were affecting my feelings. I refused to see the other side and closed my mind in stubbornness, not taking into consideration my father's pressures and responsibilities. Later I wanted to say, 'Daddy, if I'd only known!'"

Shannon doesn't excuse herself for her fault and sin. But she does point out that if only her dad could have shared his feelings, his problems, and his reasons, she might have been helped to understand and obey.

Young people, who seek a personal context for the exercise of authority, feel a deep need to know parents and teachers as persons. They want to trust and to be trusted in return. They want and need to understand us, to have us share.

Experiencing love. Earlier in the chapter, we heard Rob say about his times of conflict, "My parents always showed their love at times like these, and we soon made up."

Showing love is *the* key to youths' acceptance of authority. Where they are convinced that love is at the root of guidance and command, the way to acceptance of authority is prepared. But not every home is a home of love. Ruth writes of her home (a Christian home), "I cannot remember being told that I was loved. Nor did I receive any physical demonstrations of love. When I was 18, I left home for nurse's training. Mom wanted to kiss me good-bye. I was repelled. A child just doesn't take home, food, clothing, and education as proof of love—it's something that his parents owe him! A kiss at this time proved nothing."

Tragically, many teens are just as unsure of Christ's love as Ruth was of her parents'. Mary tells of her spiritual life in high school in words that sketch as cold, impersonal, and distant a relationship with God as Ruth knew with her parents. "The traditional expressions and concepts were a very real part of my thoughts and prayers. My active relationship with God was largely motivated by guilt about witnessing and devotions, but I did keep these up quite consistently. Often my devotions in the morning were spurred on by the thought, *What will happen if I don't*? I never doubted my salvation, only my worth. It didn't seem very significant that God loved me, because He loves everybody."

Not having a deep awareness of God's great love for her, motivated by guilt and fear of reprisal from a vast and distant authority, Mary never knew joy in Christ, or felt His guiding hand as love's touch.

But as we think of authority, isn't it true that God's Word speaks His will to us because of His love? Isn't the Gospel good news? And isn't that good news that Christ Jesus, God's Son and our living Lord, seeks to infuse the life of sinful men with a forgiveness-born love for Him and for others? Isn't everything God says to us spoken by virtue of our relationship with His Son?

Surely God's Word, that massive love letter expressing His heart's desire for us, must be read and understood as *loving* guidance; as authority, surely; but *never* impersonal, distant, or uninvolved authority. And ever, always, a personal and gently guiding Word. Our teens need this message from us.

A balanced communication of God's Word, then, never draws back from commitment to the full authority of a God who knows and speaks what is right; a God, who, in His justice and righteous character will always act in harmony with that which is right—even when it means judgment of those who reject and resist His truth. But at the same time, love and personal concern for people must always be the context within which we hear God's voice of authority through the Word.

How then, teachers, can we be any less personal, any less involved, any less loving, than the God we represent?

And how can youth fail to respond when, listening to them, sharing with them, and expressing constantly God's love, we communicate His trustworthy—and personal—Word?

GIVING YOUTH THE GROW-AHEAD

REACT

1. Recall your own teenage relationship with your parents. Did you strain toward independence and experience any conflicts at home? If so, how did you feel? What about your parents' actions helped you or made the situation more difficult?

2. What adults influenced you most as a young person? What kind of relationship did you have with those adults? Did you view them as "authorities"? What kind of authority did they try to exert?

ACT

1. Talk with the young people in your Sunday School class about their high school teachers. Ask them to name the ones they like, and do not like. Then see if your group can come up with a list of characteristics of the well-liked and disliked schoolteachers.

2. Discuss how liking or not liking a schoolteacher affects your teens. What does the relationship have to do with studies? With grades? With attitude toward the subject? With behavior in class, etc.?

3. Afterward, using the criteria your teens have developed for public school teachers, evaluate your own relationship with the young people. What have you learned about relating to teens that can help you become a better teacher?

CHAPTER FOUR
CONCERN FOR THE NOW

▶ "Inwardly," Phil recalls, "I wanted and strove for feelings of self-worth and acceptance. The popular kids in school were the smartest. So I studied.

"I noticed that the more you made people laugh, the more they accepted you. So I turned into a part-time clown. This helped others accept me, but inside I didn't accept myself.

"Wrestling provided the opportunity to develop physically. I threw myself into it and walked away with the top wrestling award the school offered. Real satisfaction came when one of the popular girls remarked, 'Boy, I sure wish I had a medal like that.'"

Talk to teens about their feelings and concerns, or listen in on their conversations, and you'll generally find that their attention seems to be focused on things that are happening to them *now*.

Sometimes a young person tries to retreat from the pressures of the "now." Tina tried to mix her fantasies with the world of daily experience, and failed. "I continued to mix my dream world—encouraged by movies, novels, and television—with the real world, and they never successfully mingled. So rather than face harsh realities of growing up and accepting the world and myself as I was, I remained in my own fixed world."

Others, unlike Tina, look for escape in drugs, alcohol, or sexual experimentation. Recently too many news headlines have featured stories of teen suicide. So even though teens today may be more aware of the future than were their counterparts of the past, and often select high school classes with a view to what they intend to study in college or do as adults, young people remain deeply concerned about the now.

Some seem to avoid the trauma of adolescence. These are teens who enter into campus or church activities for teens with enthusiasm and enjoyment. They move through experiences without apparent strain or any deep concern about who they are or who they are becoming. These young people may look back on the high school years as *really fun*, a time of enjoyment and freedom from pressure.

But to most teenagers, concern with the now goes deeper. "I had problems accepting the way I look. As in most teenagers, this tended to make me self-conscious, and I varied between feeling ugly and handsome."

And, from Mary, "I had a pretty consistently low opinion of myself. I can remember many times not being able to think of one person that I knew, including a homely, fat friend of mine, that I would not rather trade with and be her instead of me."

Life is not comfortable. There are many challenges to face, one's identity to struggle with, and other people to learn to live with successfully.

And for some young people, concern with their now

goes deeper still, even to despair. A girl from San Francisco tells of her drug culture friends, and points out, "It's a gut-level, intense way of living. Life wasn't a social, party, fun scene. Life was a search for real answers to the questions of 'Who am I? Where am I going? What is life all about?'"

No wonder youth have a concern for the now. The kids who are living on the surface, happy with their fun, are satisfied with the now. The majority, experiencing some level of uncertainty and self-consciousness and doubt, are struggling to discover and be themselves. The deeply concerned, eager for meaning, frantically demand answers—now.

Now is important. To adolescents, life is real, and now is the stuff life is made of.

Perhaps this is one of the mistakes we adults make. Perhaps we tend to look at young people and see them, not as they are, but as they *will be*. We tend to say, "I need to teach them this so they'll be prepared for college"; or, "I need to teach them this so they'll be as mature as adults." And then we can't understand it when teens don't seem to *care* about the truths we teach them for their tomorrows.

Actually, young people feel that their lives are real and earnest *now*. They feel that the problems they grapple with, the feelings, the struggle to learn and understand, the relationships they test and try to build, that *these* are what life is all about—not tomorrow.

In a way they're right. When we ignore youths' present concerns, we're saying that neither they nor their problems are real, that only their future is real and important. And this is a viewpoint that young people today simply cannot accept. They know how real their concerns are to them. They know that now is of vital concern.

GIVING YOUTH THE GROW-AHEAD

Now is important to God, too. Why? The only time we have to deal with is that little bit squeezed between past and future. It's true that "today is the first day of the rest of your life," and that how we live *today* determines what tomorrow will be like.

So we need to teach the Bible in such a way that God and eternity are brought into youths' now. We need to bring youths' present concerns into the open and then look in Scripture to discover God's guidelines. We need to help our young people discover and experience His good and perfect will *now*.

In this, of course, we need to ask how we can best prepare young people for their future. Do we do it by telling them what they will need to know then (knowing also that they will probably forget long before the future comes)? Or do we prepare them for the future by teaching them how to come to God and search His Word for guidance? Do we help them discover in their present experience that they can trust God, as they seek to live close to Christ each day? Do we prepare them by helping them learn by experience that God is able and willing to meet their every need?

To me, the answer we must give seems clear.

Youths' concern *is* focused on present experience. And the present *is* of utmost importance to a young person's development and growth. As a teacher, I need to take youths' present experiences as seriously as they do. I need to realize that their now does count, and I need to concentrate on helping my teens bring their now into harmony with God's Word and will. I need to concentrate on helping my teens experience the presence of God in their hearts and lives *now*.

Young People

I hope all I've been saying in these last chapters about

"youth" doesn't make them seem like a peculiar breed, people who are different from you and me. In fact, they're *not* really different.

They're human beings. As people, bound up in the common experience of humanity, we have far more *similarities* with the young than we have differences.

It helps me to think of youth as people. I have to remember that while the details of our lives differ, they still feel joy and pain, alienation and rejection, discouragement and enthusiasm, hope and uncertainty, just as I do. To the extent that I have such experiences (though specific causes and details differ), I can understand youth and enter their lives. And they can understand and share mine. They are people as I am.

Remembering this also helps me to overcome the common fear of youths, as though they were strange, dangerous, inscrutable. They are people. And as people they need to be loved and accepted. They need to accept themselves as God has made them, and reach out in love toward others. They need to experience God's love and know His guidance and indwelling power as they live obediently with Him. Remembering they are individuals helps me remember that I need to treat them as individuals. I need to see them as individuals I can care about and come to know, accept, understand, and share myself with.

Why, then, all these words about understanding young people? Why not simply talk of the ways they are like us and all that the likeness means in teaching?

Because there are certain characteristics of young people in our culture today that have a dramatic impact on our teaching. These make so much difference in the way we need to communicate the Word of God to them that the crucial characteristics—and their implications—must be understood.

GIVING YOUTH THE GROW-AHEAD

It is these crucial characteristics I've tried to sketch in these three chapters. Characteristics that we *must* understand because they will shape the way we teach.

What were they? Let's review them, and pinpoint just what they imply for us in our teaching ministry.

Youth identify with other young people. The attitudes and values and beliefs other teens hold and express are likely to have a great impact on individuals. So in teaching, we need to help our teens express and share their attitudes and values and beliefs. We need to avoid making Bible teaching strictly an adult-to-teen declaration. We need, in fact, to teach in such a way that the teens study and apply the Bible together, not in such a way that the teens only sit together and listen to what an adult thinks and says.

Values are communicated in relationships. This is another reason why high school and even junior high school Bible study should increasingly be a time to study and think it through together. When a group moves toward commitment, each individual is supported and encouraged in his or her own commitment. Faith then grows *with* the current of his or her particular "culture," not against that stream.

Actually, this is one reason why God gave us the church, that we might be a people linked intimately as brothers and sisters, as members of a single body, to support and encourage each other in our growth as Christians (cf. Eph. 4:16). We can help develop this kind of "church" relationship when we help our teens express and share themselves as they explore the Word and as they seek to live by the Word.

Youth are in the process of establishing their identity as individuals. In this process, they are, or will be, making decisions about the standards and principles by which they will live. Everything we know about the development of values tells us that other people have a great impact on the values we choose and on the persons we become. Yet under pressure to conform, many teens find it impossible to be themselves. They feel forced to fit the expectations of others.

Studying the Bible brings teens face to face with God's portrait of a Christian—the kind of person that, in Christ, they are called to be. Freedom to step out of the mold and be themselves—to act on self-chosen standards—is usually tied to an experience of acceptance. Knowing that others love them and accept them as they are, they don't have to pretend anymore.

Thus it's important in Bible teaching to develop a context of relationships in the class—and with individual students—that provides an experience of acceptance. Bible teaching then is an *inter-* and *deeply personal* transaction. It is not simply giving information. It is giving of yourself to reassure and love and encourage. And it is helping young people relate to each other in this same accepting, caring, Biblical way.

Youth feel a need for independence. They need to feel our respect for them as persons, our recognition of their right to make important decisions for themselves.

We show respect in a number of ways. Listening is one. Not forcing our opinions is another. We talk things over instead of demanding the right to tell.

One sign that we respect young people as maturing individuals is giving them meaningful roles in Bible study; not just "read the paragraph, please, John," but permitting John to probe a passage of Scripture and share the meaning he discovers. Certainly the person who merely "tells" young people in teaching—without listening, without involving them in study or discussion, seems (to the teens) to treat them as children, not as near adults.

GIVING YOUTH THE GROW-AHEAD

For youth, to whom the symbols of independence are so important, it's especially important that we study God's Word with them in their class—and that they not be mere "members" of our classes.

Youth have a special view of authority. They are willing to give us and what we say a hearing, but they want to test the reality of what we have to say. So we need to translate God's Word by sharing its impact on our own lives. We want to encourage teens to live the Word, and spend time in class helping them see just how the Bible passage studied will affect their lives. Classes that do not focus on the application of Bible truths, but concentrate solely on content, fail to reach teens.

Youth care deeply about their present experiences. The now is real and important to young people. So we need to stop thinking of youth as though they will be persons only when they grow older. We need to stop teaching with only their futures in mind. We need to bring God's Word to bear on their present, to help them see that God wants to be involved in their concerns, and that His Word is something they can follow and experience now. We need to concentrate on our class members' *present* relationship with Jesus Christ, to provide the very best kind of equipping for their futures.

So youth do need to be taught the Bible in special ways. Because of the way they are, we need to adjust the way we teach. *The more our teaching of the Word fits their special characteristics, the more effective our teaching will be.* And the more likely our teens will be to respond to the God who speaks to them through us.

REACT

1. Youth are preoccupied with present experiences

because the present is important to them. And what happens to them now is crucial in the kind of persons they become. What does this indicate about the sections of Scripture we need to teach them?

2. Check through the list of special characteristics of teens given in this chapter. How many of these can you see in the teens you teach? In what ways might you expect each of these to show up?

ACT

1. In Chapter 1, a number of questions were raised about teaching young people. Some of these questions can be wholly or partially answered on the basis of the youth characteristics sketched in the last three chapters. Why not read through those earlier questions and see which ones you can answer now? Try to tie your answers to one or more of the special characteristics given in this chapter.

2. The next chapters of this book will move into specific ways of communicating in class that show *how* to teach in a pattern that fits youths' needs and characteristics—and the Bible's own nature as God's Word to us. When you're satisfied that you have a grasp of the principles developed to this point, move on to these next chapters with their specific teaching hints.

CHAPTER FIVE
BUILDING MUTUAL RESPECT

▶It's time. Your teens troop into the small classroom and sit on the chairs you've arranged in a wide semicircle.

You don't know them personally yet. But you do know something of their characteristics and needs. Just watching them, listening to their chatter, you're reminded of many of the things discussed in the last three chapters. But now you're faced with another problem. You know what they're like. But what does it all mean? What do you do now? How do you communicate with them? How do you teach them God's Word?

That's what the rest of this book is about—you, in the classroom. And how what you do as a teacher affects communication—either to shut it off or to facilitate it, to hinder learning or to help learning.

We won't be thinking here about what most "teaching youth" books speak of—things like projects, teaching methods, five ways to start discussion, and so on. Not that that isn't helpful.

What we'll look at in these chapters is what you do in the classroom, and how what you do affects the learning of your teens, how you as a teacher help young people understand and respond to the Word of God.

In looking at what you do in teaching teens, it's helpful to have the goal of your teaching clearly in mind. This goal is *not* simply to help your youth know what the Bible teaches. Your goal is to help them *experience* God's truth by *responding* to Him.

The Bible itself points us to this goal. We only need think of Jesus' application of the story of the wise and foolish builders. "Everyone who hears these words of mine and puts them into practice is like a wise man" (Mt. 7:24). Or of Hebrews' stern warning, reminding us that those who heard the Word of God in the wilderness refused to obey (because of unbelief) and could not enter His rest (Heb. 3:8-19). Or James's words, "Do not merely listen to the word, and so deceive yourselves. Do what it says" (Jas. 1:22). In teaching the Bible, we're concerned with more than making sure that our students know what the Bible says (hearing). We want to help them respond (doing)!

Having this goal in mind transforms the way we teach. There are many teaching skills and methods that can effectively help learners *understand information* and "master" content. Usually methods that communicate information work apart from relationships that develop in the class. Young people and college students will learn from teachers they don't like and don't respect (who are "good" communicators of content) as well as from those they do like and respect.

51

And they prove their learning of content on tests and examinations.

But in Bible teaching, we want to go beyond communication of information, to encourage and motivate response. As a teacher you're concerned that your youth *accept* and *act on* (or, if you will, believe and obey) God's Word as well as understand it. So you need to *promote acceptance* of what is learned as well as communicate Bible information. So in these chapters we'll really be asking, How does what you do in class affect your students' understanding and acceptance of God's Word?

Ultimately, of course, a student's response to God depends on the work of the Holy Spirit. It is He who teaches us all things (Jn. 16:12-15). But the Bible also teaches us that those with spiritual responsibilities are to work *with* the Holy Spirit in His teaching ministry. It is these Biblical principles for working with the Holy Spirit, translated into the classroom and adapted to young people, that we need to understand and use.

In the following chapters, then, we'll be looking at what you, the teacher, do in the classroom, and how what you do can help your teens both to understand and to respond to God's truth.

Interpersonal Relationships
Encouraging acceptance and response is accomplished basically through interpersonal relationships. This isn't true of communicating information. Closed-circuit TV gets a message across quite well. Computer-based courses are also effective in helping learners master information. But usually when what is learned is integrated into the character and personality, something about the existing relationships has played a big part. We see this in young children when they

come home and say, "I'm going to be a teacher, like Miss Jones"; or when they say, "I hate school! My teacher is so unfair!" We see it in college students when they become excited about the subject a particular professor teaches, and want to change their major. Something about the person helped make the things he or she taught meaningful and exciting.

We have the same thing in Scripture. More than once Paul reminds the readers of his letters of how close they have been. He thanks them for their love, offers himself as an example to them, and encourages them to remember how he spent time with each one individually in stimulating his or her faith. And of course we encounter the same thing in Christ's ministry with His disciples. Those He chose to teach and train for leadership He chose "to be with him." He communicated in words that had the ring of eternal life, while His disciples, in being with Him, had "seen the Father." God's truth was communicated, and is to be communicated, in the context of relationships.

So teaching becomes an especially exciting ministry. It becomes communicating with people, personally sharing God's truth and life with others. Teaching means becoming involved with the members of your class as individuals, seeing them respond to God, as well as learn about Him. In this kind of teaching (that gains understanding of what God says and gains the response of faith in the God who speaks) and involvement, relationship is important.

And so we're back to the big question again. What do you do in class that affects your communication? What opens youths up for hear-and-do learning, and what causes resistance?

The title of this chapter gives one important clue. Teens learn better and are more likely to respond when the teacher develops an atmosphere of mutual respect. When the teachers show respect and consideration for the students, they thus earn respect and consideration in return.

Respect is, of course, an attitude. It's a basic way of looking at and testing others. And it's expressed in a variety of ways. For example, let's look into a high school class and evaluate several short scenes that show a teacher asking questions of his students.

We know, of course, that the question-and-answer method is a basic one in teaching. We ask questions to stimulate thinking and encourage participation. And certainly in Bible teaching, thinking and participation ought to have high priority. But not all questions are good questions. In fact, not all *good* questions should be asked! Let's look at these scenes and see if we can find out why.

Each of the classes is studying Jesus' statement, "My teaching is not my own. It comes from him who sent me. If anyone chooses to do God's will, he will find out whether my teaching comes from God or whether I speak on my own. He who speaks on his own does so to gain honor for himself, but he who works for the honor of the one who sent him is a man of truth; there is nothing false about him" (Jn. 7:16-18).

In the first class, these are the questions the teacher asks of his teens:

"Tim, what question led Jesus to say this? Look in verse 14."

"Christie, do you think the Pharisees wanted to do God's will?"

"Bob, whose authority did Jesus claim for His teaching?"

As you observe this class, you find that the teens do answer and give right answers. But they answer slowly and without enthusiasm, and only when called on by name.

In the second class, a different kind of question is being asked.

"I think we can draw three important conclusions from this first statement of Jesus about His teaching. What do you think the first one is? Anyone?"

"This passage gives us a vital principle for our own lives, too. Does anyone see what it is? Come on, take a chance. What do you think it is, Dawn?"

As you observe this class, you see that the teens look very blank, as their teacher raises questions and probes. They seem to resist passively her efforts to get them involved. Finally, when in seeming desperation she calls on an individual by name, the answer often comes in the form of a return question: "Is it that we need to be willing to do God's will to know it?"

In the third class, we see an entirely different pattern of questions. Here the teacher is asking things this way:

"Jesus is saying here that everything He says and does is in God's will. It's not always easy for you or me to know when something is God's will for us, but maybe we can get some help here on this. What do you see in the passage that seems to indicate principles or guidelines we might use?"

"Okay, Chad suggested that if we're always worrying about how the things we do will appear to others, we'll have a hard time doing God's will. What do the rest of you think about that? Have you ever had any experiences that help us see how this principle works?"

As you observe the kids in this third class, you see that they respond very differently than the teens in the other two. They're much more involved. They speak up more freely. And they talk *with each other*, not simply giving answers back to their teacher. Somehow, the questions this teacher used involved the kids in discussion of the Biblical text and its meaning for them.

Questions and Answers

It would be an oversimplification to say that the question technique of the third teacher was good, and that of the first two was bad. This alone can't explain the difference in the way the young people responded.

It certainly is true that we can see clear differences in technique.

In the first class, the teacher asked fact questions, which could be answered by looking for a word or phrase or other information in the text, or questions that could be answered with a simple yes or no. There was little to challenge anyone's thinking, and the pattern that developed was repetitive. Teacher asks, a student answers; teacher asks, a student answers.

In the second class, the teacher asked "guess *my* answer" questions. Each of these questions was so framed that it was clear the teacher had the "right" answer already in mind. She was asking her students to guess what that right answer was. When an answer was given, the teacher used the answer as a springboard for further talk, either correcting the student if the guess was wrong or explaining the answer if it was right.

In the third class, the teacher asked open-ended questions. She focused the attention of class members on a general area or a problem, and then asked them what they discovered and thought or felt. She was interested in *their* answers, *their* insights, and her questions led to class exploration of the Bible text and its meaning for the young people.

Technically, the last question pattern is the best, because it is designed to lead to discussion. But in actuality, what makes the difference is the attitude of the teacher toward the students that the questioning patterns reveal and communicate!

Think for a moment of the characteristics of young people. Think of their drive toward independence and of the growing mental abilities that this reflects. Or, put yourself in the student's chair for a moment. What does it say about the teacher's view of *you* when he asks, "Paul, what question led Jesus to say this? Look in verse 14"? Is the teacher treating you as a person? As an equal? As someone who is able to think and feel and do *important* things? Or are you being treated like a child? Are you respected?

The second class shows another sign of disrespect. It's a manipulatory pattern. The teacher here doesn't really care what her teenagers think or discover in the text. She's already got *the* answers sorted out—*her* answers. And her questions are designed to force the student to guess at what he or she is supposed to say! Either a "right" guess or a "wrong" guess will give the teacher an opportunity to turn on a mini-lecture. After the teens respond, you'll always see her go on to explain or to correct.

Put yourself on the receiving end of a question like this. The teacher has definitely cast herself as *the* authority. She's the one to say whether you are right or wrong. And whether you are right or wrong, she'll use your answer as a springboard for what she's got to say. You're being manipulated, and you know it. *Used*. How do you feel about it? Are you motivated to try to answer? Are you motivated to find out what the Bible is saying and how it applies to you?

The third pattern is one in which the teacher asks questions that show she *does* care about what you think and feel and experience. You can sense her respect for you as a person not only in the way the question is asked, but how she responds when you answer. She nods her head, encourages you to say more. She invites others to hitchhike on your idea. She wonders if others in the class have had experiences that fit what you've been saying.

Put yourself at the receiving end of questions like these, and you feel them very differently. The first two patterns somehow make a person feel smaller, unimportant, and they make the teacher look bigger. The last pattern makes you feel important, respected. And the teacher looks the same size you are! She's important and respected, just like you.

When the students feel respected and valued, and sense that their discoveries and experiences are important to you as a teacher, they will be much more motivated to study and respond to the Scripture you are teaching, than when they feel their ideas are unimportant and that they are being manipulated for your purposes and ends.

Control

It is easy to see how the questions a teacher asks demonstrate respect—or lack of it—for students as persons.

Of course, the issue here isn't simply the way a person asks questions. It's his or her deep-seated perception of who he or she is and who the students are, as they gather for class. A teacher's underlying attitude will always be reflected in many little ways in the teaching situation.

So before we go on, it's important to ask, What should the attitude of teachers of young people be? How should they view themselves, and how should they view their relationship with the teens?

When we think back over the three questioning

patterns we've just looked at, we can see how each teacher seemed to perceive these relationships. In the first two class scenes, the teacher was definitely casting himself or herself as the authority. He or she *controlled* the class with questions, *controlled* and *exercised authority* by reserving the right to say whether the young person's answer was right or wrong. In each of these situations, the teacher was definitely *over* the teens in teaching them what the Bible says. (In extreme cases, some teachers come across as placing themselves *over* the Bible itself!)

The impact of this pattern of relationships is to make teens feel that obeying and submitting to God's Word is obeying and submitting to the adult teacher! For *both* are cast as authority.

The third question pattern indicates a different set of relationships. In this pattern, the teacher is casting herself as an equal of the teens, not in years of experience or knowledge of the Bible, but as a person. She doesn't lord it over the high schoolers. Instead, she is genuinely interested in and respectful of their discoveries and ideas and experiences. The effect of this attitude is not to rob the teacher of respect and make her appear "smaller" in the teens' eyes. The effect is to have the teacher retain her "size" and importance, but to bring the teens up to her "size" in importance and in responsibility! This pattern brings both teacher and teens under the authority, in the teaching situation, of God's Word.

The impact of this situation is to help teens feel identification with their teacher. They can feel that obeying and submitting to God's Word is not submitting *to* the teacher, but *with* him or her! In this situation, God alone is the real Authority.

And how right this is. The Bible speaks of the

husband as head of the home, but also of husband and wife submitting to each other (I Pet. 3:1-7). The Bible speaks of respect and submission of the younger to the elder, but hastens to add that each should defer to the other and serve the other in humility (I Pet. 5:5, 6). For all of us, leader and led, teacher and taught, are under the authority of the one God, led by one Spirit who indwells and teaches us, responsible as God's children to obey and to be like our Heavenly Father.

When a teacher enters his or her class of teens and treats them with respect, encouraging them by example to submit themselves to the God of Scripture, and guiding them to look with him or her in the Word to see how to respond to God with faith's quick obedience, the class will develop a desire to *know* and to *do*. When a teacher enters his or her class of teens and treats them without respect, exhorting them from a position as adult to submit to God, controlling their study of the Bible so they will learn what *he or she* has learned, the class is most likely first of all to resent the teacher, and then to ignore the truths he or she teaches.

For, teacher, you *do* make a difference in how your class responds to God!

You can be God's instrument for good, a channel through which the Holy Spirit speaks. Or you can be a dam, blocking the flood of His living water.

REACT

1. The chapter suggests that the attitude of the teacher toward the students has a great impact on their learning and response. Have you ever experienced anything like this in your own times as a student? Or as an employee? Or in some other relationship? How important is mutual respect to *you*?

2. The chapter suggests that a teacher with a nonrespecting attitude makes it hard for teens to respond to Scripture because they will feel that they are obeying the *teacher* as well as (or instead of) God. How does an adolescent's drive for independence, described in Chapter 3, help explain this reaction?

ACT

1. The importance of response to God's Word is stressed throughout the Bible. To check it out, take a concordance and see how many times Scripture speaks of "keeping," "doing," and "obeying," God's Word. This stress in Scripture helps us fix the focus of our teaching on God's great concern—that we learn for *living*, not just for information.

2. Think through the last few classes that you have taught, and jot down all the questions you can remember having asked. What kinds of questions are they? Analyze them, using the examples of the three classes discussed in this chapter. What attitude did your questions communicate to your teens?

3. Look through your *next* Sunday's lesson, and see if there are ways that you can communicate to your teens that you see yourself as *with* them, under the common authority of Scripture.

CHAPTER SIX
STRUCTURING THE CLASS

▶In the last chapter, I suggested that a teacher needs to abandon authoritarian control of the students and the class. He or she needs to avoid that "I'm-over-you" situation that young people feel and may resent, and to communicate instead an "I'm-in-this-with-you" feeling.

But this seems to raise a problem. Bible teaching does have a goal—to help learners understand and respond to God's Word. So a teacher simply can't let a class shoot off in just any direction. The process has to be guided toward a goal—response to God. Can a teacher help his or her class reach this goal without exercising an "over you" kind of control?

When teens are in class with teachers who treat them with respect, there's little danger of their forgetting who's the adult, or of failure on their part to respect them and follow their lead.

We all know that equality doesn't mean sameness. For example, we say that "all men are created equal."

But we know there are many differences among persons. Some are more intelligent than others. Some are stronger. Some are taller, and others are better looking. Yet when we say all men are "equal" we assert something important—that each is *important*, each is valuable as a person. So each person ought to be treated with respect and given his or her full rights under the law. While we say that in Bible teaching the teacher wants to treat his or her students with respect and to communicate by an attitude that he or she stands *with* them under the authority of Scripture, we're not saying that the teacher becomes *the same as* any other member of the class. We're not saying that he or she has the same role in the class as the teens, thus losing control.

This is intuitively known and accepted by the students. They see the teacher as an adult, and *expect* him or her to take the lead. As he or she shows them respect, they will almost always respond by showing an equal respect. It's this element of mutual respect, shown by the teacher in listening and caring about what the young people think and feel, and shown by the students in looking to the teacher for guidance and leadership, that helps the class move smoothly and effectively toward attaining the learning goal.

Normally loss of control in the class stems from the teacher's failure to understand the structure of the class and his or her failure to guide it effectively toward the learning goal. Loss of control is normally *not* related to a teacher's failure to be an authority, or because he or she is too friendly with the students.

So at this point, we need to get the structure of an adolescent Bible class clearly in mind, and see the ways a teacher guides the learning of the teens toward the goal of response to God.

The Whole Process

It's only appropriate that our process for Bible teaching, like our class content, comes from God's Word itself.

As noted in the last chapter, in Scripture there are many pointers to the goal of Bible teaching. We are to be "doers of the word." We are to respond with faith—the kind of faith that acts and obeys because of its deep trust in the God who speaks to us. There are also pointers to the way we are to come to the Bible and interact with it to reach this goal. Probably no passage develops the whole process as clearly, however, as one in Colossians. This passage (Col. 1:9, 10) records a prayer of the apostle Paul for believers in the young Colossian church, a prayer that they might come to know God better and experience the fruit God's Spirit produces in human lives.

For this reason, since the day we heard about you, we have not stopped praying for you and asking God to fill you with the knowledge of his will through all spiritual wisdom and understanding. And we pray this in order that you may live a life worthy of the Lord and may please him in every way: bearing fruit in every good work, growing in the knowledge of God.

Paul's prayer shows us that this kind of growth starts with the Word. While we may speak of "knowing God's will" in a personal and private sense ("It's God's will for me to take this job," etc.), the original language makes it clear that Paul is speaking here of God's will in a public, revealed sense. Growth in our relationship with God means we must understand "that which God has willed." And today we discover God's plans and purposes in the holy Scriptures He has given us.

So our class process *must* involve helping young

people understand what God has revealed to us. Sunday School is for *Bible* teaching.

But the passage goes on to show us much about *how* we are to study and "know" the Bible. We are to know what God has willed in "all spiritual wisdom and understanding." This is more than mastery of Bible information. *Wisdom* and *understanding*, in the original languages as today, convey the idea of ability to see how information applies to daily life. A "smart" person may have a lot of information. A "wise" person knows how to use it! So in Bible teaching, we move from mastery of what the Bible says, to a consideration of what it means for life and how we use the truth we've discovered in making our daily choices and decisions. It's a five-step process that works like this:

Step One: The Bible
(Knowledge of what God has willed)

Step Two: Life Implications
(In spiritual wisdom and understanding)

Step Three: Response
(Live life worthy of the Lord)

Step Four: Fruit
(Bearing fruit in every good work)

Step Five: Know God Better
(Increasing in the knowledge of God)

The next element focuses our attention on practice. We need to act on the truths we've studied and put those truths to the test in our daily lives.

The results? Here the prayer changes from the active tenses that mark our responsibility (to know the Word, to search out its implications for our lives, and to act on them) to what the Holy Spirit does in us as we respond in faith. And that? As we act on the Word in a faith-motivated response, the Holy Spirit within us creates His fruit in all we do, and deepens our awareness of God in our personal relationship with Him.

The process that we want to guide our students through, then, involves leading them to understand what the Bible says, guiding them to spell out the life implications of what has been discovered, and motivating them to put God's truth into practice.

With this overview of the process, we can define the class structure more sharply.

First, we want to interest and motivate the students to get into the Bible. (I call this part of the process a HOOK. It establishes contact with the student by dealing with a felt need—a life need—that hooks the student's interest.)

Second, we want to help our teens discover what the Bible is saying. (I use the word BOOK to describe this step. Bible learning takes place in this section.)

Third, we want to guide our teens to explore the implications of the truth(s) just discovered (the LOOK, or Bible application to their own lives).

And fourth, we want to motivate our students to act on the truths discovered and explored; to lead them to decisions that will affect their daily lives for Christ (TOOK). We want them to make life responses.

Points for Guidance

Understanding this four-step process gives clues as to how you can maintain control and guide your class toward Bible study's real goal. What happens in the classroom should be directly related to the process shown in Colossians; the teacher's role is one of guiding the students *into* the Word, to *understanding* the

Word, to exploring the *implications* of the Word, and then to a living of daily life *by* the Word.

Initiating the HOOK—*the life need.* This first part of the process has no direct parallel in the Colossians passage. Rather its nature is defined by the psychology of the learners.

In looking at young people in the early chapters of this book, we saw that they have a particular concern for the now, that they care about the experiences they are having, the problems they face, the situations they find themselves in at home and at school. These things are *rightly* their concern; what happens to people during the adolescent years does make a difference in personality and character, in the kind of people they become. So young people *need* (as well as *want*) to study the Bible as it relates to their personal experience.

One of the most important things a teacher can do to motivate adolescent Bible study is to tie the study to a need or problem that students can identify as their own. Thus the first part of class will usually be given to raising a question that teens themselves ask, or to exploring an issue that is important to them. Many different methods are adaptable for use as a HOOK. You might tell a story about a teen facing a decision, and then leave the question, "What should he or she do?" open for discussion. You might simply put a challenging statement on the board and have your teens react to it. You might give a quiz that probes for attitudes on your subject. Whatever method you use, your purpose is to help your teens *feel* this issue as their own, as something interesting and important. Often your teacher's guide will help you on this point, but be aware of your kids' special concerns—and use them to personalize your lessons.

When their concern has been developed, you've reached a second crucial point where your guidance is needed.

Transition to the BOOK. Your purpose in raising the initial "hooking" issue was to help the teens realize that what they will be studying in Scripture is something that is important to them. When interest and concern have been aroused, you need to focus that interest and use it to motivate study of the Bible.

In effect, you need to say something like, "Today we're going to look into a passage of Scripture that helps us see how to solve this problem (or make this decision, or understand how to handle this situation, etc.)." The transition statement from HOOK to BOOK, then, specifies the learning goal for the lesson.

If you've been successful in the initial HOOK activity, then you'll have motivated teens, ready for purposeful Bible study.

Involving in the BOOK. In view of high schoolers' and collegians' developing mental powers, it's usually desirable to have them dig out truths by direct study of the Bible. A variety of approaches and methods is available, from the use of buzz groups to individual outlining or paraphrasing. The method is not the most important thing. What is important is that the teacher direct the attention of the teens to Scripture and help them ask the right questions of the text to discover what God is communicating in that portion of His Word.

Of course, it's not wrong to lecture or simply *tell* the young people what a passage teaches. Sometimes, when time is a factor or you've planned an extended discussion of implications, you'll want to take shortcuts like this. But usually, remembering the ability of young people to think and probe, you'll want to involve them

in personal discovery of Bible truths, particularly a
when you do this, you'll be equipping them with k
how for studying the Bible on their own.

Exploring through the LOOK—*the Bible applica*
When your class members have an understanding
the content they have been studying, guide them t
spell out its implications.

This is a very difficult process to activate and gui
but a crucial one. The reason it's difficult seems to
that in our culture all of us (youth and adults as well)
resist translating principles or generalizations into
concrete terms. It's easy to say from the study of a
passage, "We need to *want* to do God's will," or "We
need to think first about what will honor God." The
principles are there, in the text. But if we ask, What
does that mean in terms of my life or my experience?
Where do kids on campus have a rough time in putting
God's honor first? Why do we really hesitate to want
God's will?—then we're forcing ourselves to think in
concrete, bluntly practical terms.

But this is what wisdom demands—translating the
abstract or the principle into daily life implications. And
then moving into life to experience the principle by
putting what we've explored into practice.

In this part of the teaching process, then, a teacher
needs to keep probing to help the teens think in
concrete terms. "But what does this truth mean to a
teen in this kind of situation? What does it mean to a
guy in school? What decisions or choices might be
affected if we understand and live by this truth? How?
Why?"

In this process, it's particularly important to ask
"open" questions that honestly seek another person's
ideas and feelings. For it's in discussion of the meaning
of God's Word for their lives that your high schoolers

will be most influenced by one another and most likely to see areas of their own lives to bring into harmony with God's revealed will and ways.

Motivating by the TOOK. This final "life response" part of the process encourages students to decide to put into practice truths studied. Normally, practice of a Bible truth happens outside of class. Few truths studied will be immediately applied in the classroom. So the teacher is concerned with guiding the students to see what decisions they face that involve response to the truths studied, and to explore results of choosing to follow—or ignore—God's path. And you, as a teacher, are concerned with supporting and encouraging your teens to step out in faith and act on God's Word.

At each of these points, then, special teaching skills are needed. We'll look at some of these skills as we move on to other chapters in this book. But for now, the main thing to note is that the *process* controls the class—not the teacher—and that the controlling process is revealed in God's own Word.

The teacher who understands the process has a good chance of developing the skills needed to guide youth into and through the process. Without an understanding of the process, no form of control is likely to facilitate successful learning, if learning is viewed as doing, not merely knowing, God's Word.

To review:

HOOK involves teens in an issue/problem *important* to them.
▶ It gets attention.
▶ It focuses on a life need youth can feel.
▶ It involves teens in discussion of the issue.

TRANSITION shows teens that the Bible study to follow is *relevant* to them.

▶ It states a learning goal.
▶ It promises solution or help with the issue.

BOOK gets teens to discover God's point of view in Scripture.
▶ It usually involves direct Bible study.
▶ It seeks to *understand* what God says.

LOOK involves teens in discussion of the meaning of Bible truths learned, the Bible application.
▶ It keeps discussion practical.
▶ It encourages youths' open expression of ideas and feelings.
▶ It moves to *real-life* situations.

TOOK motivates decision to respond.
▶ It focuses on the need for making a life response.
▶ It explores the results of choices.
▶ It supports and encourages teens who want to respond.

A Blend
At this point, then, we have moved toward a sharper understanding of the teacher's role in communicating God's Word.

In the first place, the teachers need to treat students with respect, showing in the questions they ask and the way they listen and respond that they are persons with the students, submitting themselves as they encourage teens to submit to God's authority through His Word. Showing respect is crucial in the classroom, for many reasons. We've seen some. Respect helps a young person feel freer to express himself or herself and motivates participation. Respect lets a person feel the teacher is supporting and encouraging him or her to respond to God, not demanding that he or she knuckle under to the teacher's authority as an adult. Respect helps young people feel and accept responsibility for their own actions and choices, and adds further motivation for response to God.

An understanding of structure helps us see just how important freedom to participate is. Teen participation is particularly vital at the beginning of the lesson (to help them become involved in and feel the importance of the issue or problem you've chosen for launching the Bible study). It is utterly necessary at the LOOK step, for it is youth who best know their lives and their needs. Only as you help your young people express and explore the meaning of truth for their own lives will you be likely to apply truth to just that point in life to which the Holy Spirit wishes to speak.

Secondly, the teacher needs to be sensitive to process and structure, and to know how to guide students at crucial points in the process to move toward Bible teaching's goal. Mastery of the process and structure of the class is vital to becoming a truly good teacher. While some teach this way intuitively, understanding of what is happening and why can help you become more effective in your ministry with teens.

REACT

1. Succeeding chapters will explore in more depth what happens at various crucial stages in the teaching-learning process. But it's helpful to get the overall structure in mind now. One way to begin is to think back over the last class or two that you have taught and try to diagram or trace its structure. Where did you start? Where did you move? Where did your class end?

2. Many curricula for youth today adopt the process I've described in this chapter. Look over your own materials. Can you see this kind of process there?

ACT

1. Another use of the structure is to help in planning your lessons. Why not "rough out" on a sheet of paper the lesson you'll be teaching next Sunday to your teens? Remember, the methods you use should be chosen in view of your *purpose* in the activity. List your purposes in a column on the left, with room for you to jot down on the right what you will do (questions, illustrations, etc.) and what you expect from the teens as you guide. Use the following to test your purposes at each step:

   ▶ HOOK: Does it get attention? Does it focus on an issue students can feel? Does it involve them in discussing the issue?

   ▶ TRANSITION: Does it set a learning goal? Does it promise a solution or help?

   ▶ BOOK: Does it help them *understand* what the Bible teaches?

   ▶ LOOK: Does it keep discussion practical? Does it encourage open expression of ideas and feelings? Does it move to real-life situations and experiences?

   ▶ TOOK: Does it focus on the need for decision? Does it explore the results of teens' choices? Does it support and encourage teens who want to respond?

2. Other books on teaching can enrich your understanding and skill. Why not check them out at your local Christian bookstore?

   My own *Creative Bible Teaching* (Moody Press, 1979) is used as a textbook in many Bible colleges and seminaries, and goes into detail on how to use the teaching process I've outlined in this chapter.

An excellent book that will help you see a variety of exciting and effective methods to get your young people involved in group Bible study is Marlene LeFever's *Creative Teaching Methods* (David C. Cook Publishing Co., 1985).

CHAPTER SEVEN
TEACHING TO MEET NEEDS

▶The word *relevant,* which appeared in the last chapter, was much overworked in the 1970s. But it is important. Relevance insists that what the Bible communicates is important to youth, that the Bible speaks to their problems and to their needs.

But relevance also has a subjective aspect. It implies that a person feels that something is important to him or her. When these two elements (something that is important, and something that seems important) come together, real learning is likely to take place.

Often in books on teaching or in articles on Christian education, we read of *teaching to meet needs.* The writers suggest that you, the teacher, remember that you're teaching individuals—not simply "a lesson." It's a good reminder to heed. In making this suggestion, Christian education writers aren't downgrading the importance of the Bible or of lesson content. Instead, they're reminding us that for meaningful learning, we need to consider the *learners* and come to know them at least as well as we know our *content*. For we communicate the Bible best when we relate its content to a need learners see as their own. It's in this setting— where the teacher knows both the Bible and the students, and brings the truth of the Word to bear on the needs of the learner—that real learning is most likely to take place.

So we do need to remember that we're teaching individuals, and we do need to know these individuals well enough to connect their needs with the Bible as we teach.

Actually, it's easy to see how such a knowledge of our students' feelings and concerns can vitalize a class. In the last chapter we noted that the first part of the teaching process, the HOOK, is designed to capture teens' interest by bringing up an issue that they can feel is important to them. The better we know our teens and their concerns, the better we'll be able to identify a life need that involves and motivates them in the Bible study. Knowing needs that our young students feel *as* needs is vitally important in effective teaching.

Discovering Needs
There are a number of ways that teachers can learn their students' needs. In thinking of the different sources of information, it's important to note just *whose* perception of needs is involved. That is, to keep in mind just who "feels" the need that the youth do, or are said to, have. Here are several sources from which we can learn of teen needs, and the kind of information a teacher can expect from each source:

Source: Psychologists, sociologists, other professionals. These people tend to report general characteristics of the group. ("Youths as a class are identity oriented," for example.) These characteristics are true of many individual youths, but not necessarily all the time.

Source: Teachers, adult leaders. They see needs in the behavior of a group of teens in the classroom situation. ("These kids just aren't interested enough.") Who feels these needs as "important to me"? Primarily, the teachers themselves!

Source: Parents, close adult friends. These persons reveal teens' needs and weaknesses seen in behavior over time in various situations. ("He really needs to develop a sense of responsibility.") Who feels these needs as "important to me"? Primarily the parent or other adult *for* the young person.

Source: Teenage friends. They report needs and weaknesses seen in behavior or shared by the individual. ("John feels he's not given enough freedom at home.") The individual teen, subject to the interpretations of friends, feels these needs are important.

Source: The teens themselves. Teens express their own feelings and thoughts. ("No, it's just that I'm not sure I'm ready for freedom; I'm a little afraid!") Teens feel these needs themselves—*now!*

Thus we see that there are many sources from which teachers can get insights into the needs of young people. The information they gain can range from ideas about general characteristics of the age group at a particular point in time in a particular culture (the kind of thing we covered in Chapters 2-4), to specific information on how individual young people feel *now*.

In a sense, while each "need reporter" is different from the others, the sources can be reduced to two primary types. We can get information about young people's needs from *other* people or from the *young people* themselves.

Obviously, each of these sources can give us accurate and important information. Each can give us true information and reveal real needs that young people (the teens in your class, for instance) actually have. And so we want to take advantage of all these sources of information in getting to know our students and in seeking to understand and appreciate them.

However, going to others for information is risky. The main problems with using other people as our primary source of information about a youth's needs are that (1) the needs discovered may not be needs a particular individual has just now; (2) the needs discovered may reflect needs the reporter has rather than needs the young person has; and (3) the needs discovered may be needs the young person actually has but may not be needs he or she feels are "important to me."

In one sense, any needs that we deduce from observing behavior or that we discover through another person's report are somewhat suspect. In the last analysis, people themselves have to tell us what is going on inside them (what their feelings and thoughts and reasons for their behavior are). Only when they share things like this can we truly understand them or really *know* their needs—that "what's important to me *now*" stuff that successful teaching seeks to relate God's Word to. When we plan a lesson HOOK on the assumption that our class members will *feel* a need that we have observed, with the same intensity or concern that we feel it, we're likely to have a disappointing lesson! We pull learners into the lesson by focusing on a life need that is important to them—not one we think *should* be important to them.

Don't presume that we're limited in initiating our lesson to topics that the kids seem to care about at the moment. In fact, many HOOKS are designed to create awareness of a need the teens aren't conscious of at class time. But when we do this (attempt to create awareness of a need) we should be conscious of what we're trying to do and be aware of the fact that it will take time and skill to help our teens truly *feel* such a need as important to them.

Actually, then, when we work to meet needs using only information about our young people that has come from others, we're like hunters stalking game at night instead of during the day. The information we have sheds a dim light on the scene, and so we're not shooting entirely blind. We're more likely to hit our target than when we have *no* idea of what youths' needs are. But still we're likely to be deceived by shadows into shooting at game that isn't there. And we'll have far too many misses.

But we don't have to teach in the dark. We can come to understand our students' needs as they themselves feel them. How? By encouraging our teens to reveal their needs to us and to one another!

When this happens, a flood of light is shed on the classroom, and we're able to keep both the Word and our students in clear focus. When we have this kind of knowledge of where our students are, we're able to help them discover the relevance and reality of God's Word with exciting and life-changing impact.

Encouraging Self-Revelation

It seems unrealistic to many teachers to expect their teens to reveal their needs to them or to other teens.

Yet the Bible shows that this is a very basic thing in a Christian's relationship with others. As members of one body, and thus intimately related as brothers and sisters in Christ, believers are to share their lives so that "if one part suffers, every part suffers with it; if one part is honored, every part rejoices with it" (I Cor. 12:26). Christians are called to love one another, and in love to carry each other's burdens (Gal. 6:2). This command lays an obligation on the burdened believer to share as well as on the rest to care. And as believers, we are to welcome weaker and newer brothers, to encourage and build them up, not to judge them for their failures (Rom. 14).

The Bible, then, insists that Christians come out from behind their masks to speak truthfully to their fellow believers. It is vital, if we are to stimulate each other's faith, forgive each other, and bear one another's burdens in full awareness of our oneness in Christ, that we learn to express ourselves honestly and trustingly to each other.

The idea, then, that we should find out our teens' needs and discover what is important to them through their sharing with us is in essential harmony with the Bible's teachings about Christ's church. We shouldn't hesitate to encourage teens to express their feelings and their problems, or to share their experiences. We should do everything we can to create an atmosphere in class where young people feel free to be, and to express, themselves.

When will a teen feel this freedom? While there are many factors that keep people from expressing their real feelings and needs to others, the root problems are two: a lack of trust, and uncertainty that others really care.

It's easy to see why people hesitate to reveal themselves when they're afraid someone in the group is likely to spread the story around, or when they're afraid that members of the group will look down on them and show contempt for them because of their weaknesses. And in many groups it's true: one can't trust others. Only when young people or adults feel they can trust others in the group not to reject them will they feel free to reveal their real thoughts and feelings.

One factor that builds trust in a group is awareness that others really care about us as individuals—that they're not just curious, but that they're *concerned*. Care can be observed in many ways. People who care listen when a person shares; if the person is glad, they show their gladness for him or her. If the person is troubled, their faces show concern. They talk *to* the person, not *about* him or her. Care is shown outside the class, too. Some speak encouragement during the week; others will say, "I'm praying for you this week." Most, when they see the person who shared, will ask how things are going. There's a genuine concern for other people and the feeling that each person is important to others.

As I've said, this atmosphere of trust and concern is one the New Testament speaks of often. The Bible calls it "fellowship," and in many passages, defines the love we can have for each other by the practical ways that love is expressed. So it's important for the teacher of teens to know that one of his or her most important tasks is to build the classroom group toward the experience of this New Testament fellowship! When young people begin to sense such a relationship of fellowship in the classroom, they will quickly and freely express themselves and share their needs with you and others. And knowing the needs, you'll be able to *teach* to the needs, and discover an eager readiness for study of God's Word.

How can a teacher work toward a fellowship

relationship? Few high school (or adult) classes today are experiencing the kind of fellowship that creates trust and concern and frees each class member to share his or her needs with the others. One of the reasons for this is that few teachers are aware that building such a fellowship is a part of their teaching task. Too many Sunday School teachers have a very limited view of teaching. To them it's simply teaching the lesson or getting the Bible information across. But as we saw earlier, the ministry of teaching is a ministry of *communicating* God's Word. And *communicating* means helping your students experience God's truth by responding to Him. Gaining response involves both helping the learner understand the Bible's teaching and motivating him or her to accept and act on what has been learned.

So, as acceptance of what is learned is intimately related to the quality of relationships in the learning setting, the teacher has to pay close attention to his or her relationship with the class and to relationships between members of the class! The teacher *starts* to develop the atmosphere of mutual respect in the class. The teacher *continues* to develop the right kind of atmosphere for learning by sharing himself or herself with the students, and thus beginning to develop an atmosphere of sharing (fellowship) in the class!

The Bible says much about the role of the spiritual leader as example. "Be imitators of me, just as I also am of Christ," Paul says to one of the churches. Paul tells Timothy to be an example to those under his care, and to pay attention to his life and teaching.

Life and teaching go together in Scripture, for the life the teacher lives is to be in full harmony with, and to demonstrate the truth of, the Scripture he or she teaches.

So when it comes to first steps toward the building of a fellowship relationship in the classroom, it's clear the teacher must be the one to take them. If you expect your teens to express their needs to you, you will want to show them how by expressing your needs to them. If you expect your teens to share their joys with you, you'll need to share your joys with them. And if you expect them (as the Bible says you must!) to share their burdens so you can bear the burdens with them, then you need to provide an example by sharing your burdens with them.

This, then, gives us some insights into how a teacher goes about building that fellowship atmosphere in which teens feel free to express their needs, enabling you to teach the Bible to meet their needs.

First, establish an atmosphere of mutual respect by treating your students with respect.

Second, show a genuine interest in your students, and show that you care about each of them.

Third, begin to develop trust and freedom of expression in the group by demonstrating your trust in sharing yourself and your burdens and joys.

The example you provide by your own honesty and self-revelation in the classroom will, over a period of time, be the key that provides the freedom your teens need to share themselves and their needs with you and one another. It will be the key that opens the door to true fellowship.

Is Self-Revelation Safe?

There's always some hesitation about the risk necessarily involved in speaking out honestly and revealing oneself. Adults who teach or work with youth are likely to feel particularly hesitant. They wonder just how teens will react to sharing from an adult. Will they lose confidence in the teacher if they find he or she has problems, too? Will they reject the offer of closer friendship and relationship?

In answering this kind of questioning and concern, there are several things to remember.

Self-revelation is God's way for His people. The verses I quoted earlier in this chapter, and many other passages, indicate that God *expects* His children to draw closer to each other in genuine love. And this drawing near necessarily involves sharing our lives with one another, even as genuine love means becoming involved with other people.

And, since God is the One who has shown us the importance of sharing ourselves with one another, as teachers of God's Word you and I want to take the lead in living it.

Revelation of your weakness does not reflect on God. This is something many adults worry about. "If my class sees that I'm not perfect, that I have needs and problems, too, how will they trust God as I'm trying to teach them to do so? Won't they feel that what I'm saying is all phony if they find out that I still have problems, too?"

Not really.

Even the apostle Paul had to admit that he hadn't "arrived" as a Christian. He didn't hesitate to admit his failings. Yet in admitting his failings, he also revealed that he was committed fully to Christ and that he was experiencing God's grace in forgiveness and God's power to enable him to live far beyond his natural resources as a human being.

And it's the same with us. The Gospel's good news is not that you and I are perfect people and have no problems after coming to know Christ. The Gospel's good news is that even though without Christ we can do nothing, *in* Christ we have both forgiveness when we fail and fresh strength from His Spirit to succeed. When we live honestly before our teenage students, we let them see the Gospel at work. We let them see that Christ is at work in us, and that He can work in them, too, freeing them to accept forgiveness and to experience power for a new life, as they live close to Jesus Christ.

On the other hand, phoniness—unwillingness to be ourselves with others—can reflect negatively on God and give others a false impression of what He is like. And when we hide ourselves from others behind masks of self-righteousness, we join hands in company with the Pharisees—not with Christ's other disciples.

Self-revelation doesn't lead to loss of youths' respect. In fact, the reverse is true. Young people tend to view honesty as a strength. They admire the person who is willing to be himself or herself, but lose respect for the person who seems phony to them—unwilling to admit any faults or failings.

So we can afford to live honestly with our young people and to share ourselves with them. This *is* God's way for living with other people. It's in full harmony with Christ's Gospel. And it earns us the respect and appreciation of those we teach.

Finally, in living this way before them, we help our teens accept the important and necessary risk of revealing themselves to us. When we know them and understand their needs, we can be the most effective teachers of all. For then we can teach persons— bringing into intimate contact the Word of God and the young people who need to hear it and to do it.

REACT

It's always helpful to check out your own awareness of

your class members' needs. One way is to list each of your teens by name, then jot down what you know of each and the source from which you got your information or impression. If little or no information has come from the teen or his or her classmates, chances are you'll have a very inadequate knowledge of your young people's needs.

ACT

1. Look over the lesson you'll be teaching next Sunday, and think it through in terms of your own life and experience and needs. Look particularly for implications of the truth you'll be studying for your own life. And begin now to act on relevant truths.

2. At the end of the week, just before you teach, think through your experience with the lesson truths, and see if there is something you've learned or experienced or discovered about yourself that you can share with your teens. The important thing in sharing, remember, is being honest and open in what you express.

   This kind of sharing on your part sets the example for your students and can lead to a similar sharing from them.

CHAPTER EIGHT
DEVELOPING ATTITUDE TOWARD SCRIPTURE

▶Many Christian young people look on the Bible as important—even vital, but somehow not as meaningful to them as it should be. They take stabs at having personal devotions and read it sporadically. Yet the Scriptures don't come across to them as vital, exciting, and life changing. They accept the Bible as God's Word, but they haven't yet experienced it as God's personal Word to them.

The teacher of teens thus has a great opportunity—the chance to help young people discover that the Bible is exciting and relevant to them, the chance to launch youth on a lifelong and ever-deepening study of Scripture.

To some young people, the Bible seems to speak in a very negative tone of voice. They hear it with the same demanding insistence that they hear a nagging adult demanding that they conform to adult standards. When the Bible seems to speak with this kind of authority— the kind we saw in Chapter 3, which young people resent and reject—motivation for Bible study is low. Even young people who accept Scripture as God's Word find themselves fighting something deep inside when they try to read it and respond.

Scripture itself explains this reaction: "The sinful passions aroused by the law were at work in our bodies, so that we bore fruit for death" (Rom. 7:5). Like the little boy whose mother told him not to touch the cookies, the no makes us want all the harder!

But the Christian young person is in a new relationship to God. "But now, by dying to what once bound us," Paul goes on to say, "we have been released from the law so that we serve in the new way of the Spirit, and not in the old way of the written code" (Rom. 7:6). And when we discover in Scripture God's Word of Gospel (rather than law), our whole attitude toward God's Word changes, and our resistance to its authority collapses.

Remember the two ways of viewing authority described in Chapter 3? In many ways God's authority through the Word is exercised in just those ways that youths can most appreciate and respond to!

God speaks in love. This is a great unquestionable truth of our faith. We can trust the love of the God who gave His Son for us. His love has been proven once for all. And so when we read the Bible, we must hear in every word God's great love for us.

This is no distant, impersonal Word from an authority who cares more about His rules than about people. This is a deeply personal Word from our God who has drawn close to us in Christ and who invites us to draw closer to Him. He, through His Holy Spirit, is deeply involved in our lives; He lives with us and within us!

God speaks with competence. This is another exciting thing about the Bible. God knows what is helpful for us and what will harm us. He created our world and the principles by which it runs. He knows the human personality and how we must respond to life and to others in order to live meaningful and joyful lives.

And it's this that the Bible is communicating to us. God is letting us know what we and our world are really like. He's telling us about Himself and how we can live close to Him. We can't see our way in life clearly; our thoughts and ideas are cluttered by the twisted and competing values of our sinful human culture. But God can see our way; He knows what's helpful and what harms, what's right for us and what's wrong.

Actually, His laws and principles for living are just expresssions of what is right (this is always helpful for us!) and what is wrong (this is always harmful!), in this world He has created and knows so well.

God's words can be experienced. This is the last test of God's authority. It can be demonstrated and found to work in human experience. The Bible says it this way: "Do not conform any longer to the pattern of this world, but be transformed by the renewing of your mind. Then you will be able to test and approve what God's will is" (Rom. 12:2). And so God invites us to put His will to the test, and in the testing discover for ourselves that God's will is good and pleasing and perfect.

When young people sense the tone in which the Word speaks, and clear away from their thinking and feeling the overtones of stern, impersonal, demanding law, a significant change comes in their attitude toward the Word. And when they begin to experience the Word of God, discovering the love with which God speaks and the guidance into a meaningful life the Word provides, their willingness to respond to God's Word and eagerness to know will grow.

Coming to Know the Word

But response to God's guidance in Scripture depends on more than our attitude toward Scripture. It depends on knowing what the Bible says! In the next chapter, we'll look at some of the ways you can help your students view the Word correctly and respond to it. In the rest of this chapter, we need to think of how you as a teacher can help your teens discover what the Bible really says.

In this last sentence I used the word *discover*. I want to emphasize it, because it is an important word, a word that gives us a key to helping teens come to know the Bible personally and well.

In an earlier chapter, we looked at youths' sense of need to feel independent, to be viewed as responsible, to take responsibility for themselves. Often this need is felt and independence demanded long before a young person is ready for it. But when it happens, it becomes the responsibility of parents or other adults to help the young person develop the ability to live responsibly as an independent individual.

This is particularly true for the Sunday School teacher. When many of your class members were younger, their teachers (and their parents) *told* them Bible stories, and *told* them what the Bible said and meant. A few years from now they will be adults, and everyone will expect them to be able to study the Bible for themselves! But where will they learn? How will they be helped to make the transition from listeners to what others say the Bible says, to studiers of the Bible itself?

For many reasons, adolescence is *the* time of transition, the time of preparation for adult roles. For one thing, youths' growing mental powers give them the ability to think things through. For another, youths are at a time of life where they increasingly make significant choices that their parents cannot control. So they *need* to seek God's guidance in Scripture *now*. And finally, youths' sense of need for independence and responsibility makes them resist the adult "teller" and reach eagerly for guided responsibility. Teens are ready to learn how to study and know the Word.

There are other reasons, too. For example, things that are discovered for oneself are remembered longer than things one is told; things discovered seem more important to the discoverer than the same things told by an adult. Young people are *able* to discover what the Bible says for themselves, and young people will respond *better* when they are guided to discovery than when they are "told."

We need, then, to raise this question: "How can you teach in a 'discovery' way?"

'Discovery' Teaching

In teaching teens to discover and understand Scripture for themselves, you need to remember that they are in a time of transition. They're ready to dig out truths, but not ready to do it alone. As the teacher, you need to accept responsibility to structure a setting that will guide them to discovery, and enable them to dig into the Word successfully. The particular kinds of help you need to give young people involve making sure that there is a specific *goal* for the study, that you know *what to look for*, that they have a *method* for the Bible search that will ensure their search is successful, and finally, helping to *organize* the results so that what has been learned can be seen to be meaningful.

Probably the best way to see what each of these tasks of yours involves is to think through discovery patterns for the study of Romans 8:18-30. You may want to take a moment to look the passage over before reading on.

Overview of the passage. In this passage Paul explores the fact that, in this world of change, decay, and disappointment, we have hope for a very different kind of future. But the hope *is* future; God's purpose in us and in His creation has not been realized yet. Subject then as we are to so many limitations, how do we bring meaning out of a present that leads others to despair? How do we maintain hope?

Paul's answer is that the Spirit of God within us maintains hope, by helping us in our present limitations, by giving us a view of God's plan for us and His creation, and by sharing with us the exciting truth that all that happens to us now fits into His very special plan for us. God is at work *now,* shaping you and me to bear the family likeness of His Son!

Christians, then, can look around at a complex and apparently out-of-control world, burdened with pollution and overpopulation and seared by war and hatred, and believe confidently that God will change the whole creation. And Christians can look within, at their failures and weaknesses and empty efforts to be all they want to be, and assert that their lives have meaning—for they see evidence of Christ's power and Christ's Spirit at work changing them. There is meaning to life. Life has purpose and goal and direction—and hope.

Here's a process you could use to help teens discover truths in this passage:

DEVELOPING ATTITUDE TOWARD SCRIPTURE

1. *Set the learning goal:*
   a. How to handle failure and frustrations
   b. How to decide whether life today can really have purpose and meaning

2. *Provide clues to what to look for:*
   a. Causes, results, resources
   b. "Hopes," goal, and purpose

3. *Suggest a method for search:*
   a. Outline
   b. Paraphrase
   c. Word study
   d. Study chart

4. *Help organize reports:*
   a. Discussion
   b. Group reports
   c. Summary

Setting the learning goal. The effective teacher, as we've seen earlier, does not just plunge students into Bible study and expect them to be motivated or interested. The teacher needs to help them feel a concern for an issue or question that the Bible study will probe. And so he or she structures a HOOK, some activity to make the teens aware of the issue the passage deals with and to help them feel it as relevant to them.

In this passage, as in most, the Scripture provides insight into more than one issue or problem. So the study will be slanted to the issue or problem that is most important to the most young people in the class. For instance, if yours is a class of younger teenagers, kids who are often frustrated by their own failures to live up to their ideals and/or reach their goals, you might plan a HOOK activity to help them explore their experiences with such failures, and then set as a learning goal: "Today let's study a passage of Scripture that helps us see how we can handle our failures and frustrations." You have established a life need.

If you have older teens or college students who are troubled by social and world problems, and are aware of the despair many feel about trying to solve them, you might structure a HOOK activity that helps them express this concern, and then set as a learning goal: "Paul deals with the same issues in Romans, and raises the question of whether, in view of the decay all around, life can really have purpose and meaning. Let's see if his answers can help us."

In each of these cases, the learning goal was set in view of the needs and concerns of the class and in view of what the Bible passage teaches.

In Sunday School Bible teaching, being sensitive to the needs and concerns of students and being aware of what God's Word teaches about them, is a responsibility of the teacher. This responsibility is met when a learning goal is set that matches needs with the teaching of God's Word.

Providing clues. There are many ways to help your students search a Bible passage effectively. But each will point to significant elements in the passage and help the teens identify them.

For instance, for the first class (handling frustrations) you might provide an outline of the passage, asking the teens to study each section and see what ideas it contributes. The outline itself organizes the study for them and provides the necessary clues:

1. Creation itself falls short (8:18-25).
2. We have serious limitations (8:26-27).
3. Things don't work out as we wish (8:28-30).

Or, you might ask students to look through the passage for causes and results of failures—and then look through it again to see what resources the passage suggests the believer has to help handle the tendency to fail.

A third method would be to list a series of guide questions:

1. Why do we (and all things!) experience frustrations?
2. Is there any hope? Why?
3. What is being done about our failings *now?*
4. What is going to come out of even our greatest frustrations and failures?

If you are teaching the second class (meaning and purpose), you would provide other clues to help the students see how the passage speaks to this issue. You might, for instance, suggest a word study: "Underline every occurrence of the word *hope* and study the context to see what Paul says about it."

Or you might ask your teens to work from the passage to complete a chart. The chart could show the status of both believers and creation under the following headings:

1. Present condition
2. Present hope
3. Direction in which moving
4. Conclusions (our attitudes)

Or, you might ask your teens to outline the passage by summarizing in their own words each important thought.

In all of these ways you give your teens direction for their study, and help them discover what the Bible is teaching as it relates to their lesson's learning goal.

Providing a method. This responsibility often

overlaps with defining what the teens are to look for. For usually when one says *what* to look for, one also says *how*. For instance, in saying, "Look for the appearance of the key word *hope* and look in the context to discover what Paul says about it," we not only specify what to look for but also how to do it.

The same is true with the study chart already suggested. In setting up the categories on the chart, we have shown the teens both what to do and how to do it.

It's not always true, however, that telling what to look for will show our students how. We may tell our young people to try to find answers to a series of questions (*what to do*) and then add, "Probably the best way here is to paraphrase the passage with the questions in mind. That is, read what the Bible says, and try to put it in your own words. Let's try it, and see how much paraphrasing can help."

There are times when you'll want to add other variations of method. For instance, sometimes you'll want to have teens take eight or ten minutes to study the passage alone, jotting down their observations on a sheet of paper. At other times you'll want to divide the class into buzz groups of three to six teens to study together. And sometimes you'll have the whole class study together, with each sharing observations and one recording each finding on the chalkboard.

Methods of study, then, will vary according to the passage studied, what you want the young people to discover, the size of your class, and the amount of time you have available. So you will want to give your teens guidelines on how to do their study as well as guidelines on what to look for.

Organizing results. When teens search the Scriptures for personal discovery, it's important that the results of their study be shared and discussed. Charts and outlines like the ones given in this chapter not only help young people know what to study, but also help them present their findings in an organized way. Still, it will be your task as teacher to suggest how results are shared—reports from study groups, general discussion, working together to complete a "master chart" for the whole group, and so on. It will also be your task either to summarize the learnings of the group or lead them to make summary statements—generalizations about "what we have learned."

Goal of Discovery Teaching

A major concern of discovery teaching is, of course, that the young people in the class might understand what the Bible passage they are studying teaches. This is always important, for we only know how to respond to God when we understand what He is saying to us.

Discovery teaching gives a great advantage here. For when the teens in a class are involved in digging out the meaning of a passage for themselves—actively involved in a guided search of the Word—they are far more likely to grasp what Scripture teaches than when they merely listen to another person tell them. And when teens express the results of their study, you get a very clear insight into their understanding and an opportunity to clarify and correct misunderstandings.

But perhaps the most important thing about discovery teaching of the Bible is its long-range impact. For you are not only teaching your teens the content of specific passages of Scripture, you are teaching them how to go to God's Word for themselves and discover what He is saying to them. This is vital.

This is equipping them to live as mature and maturing Christians, in dependence on God, constantly feeding and growing on His Word.

GIVING YOUTH THE GROW-AHEAD

REACT

1. Many of the ideas touched on in this chapter (the tone of voice of Scripture, methods for study of the Bible) are developed in my book, *Creative Personal Bible Study* (Zondervan, 1987). If you want to go deeper into this subject, you may wish to obtain a copy from your local bookstore.

2. It's clear that what we've been thinking of in this chapter corresponds to the BOOK element of lesson structure. You may want to quickly review that section of Chapter 6 to fit the discovery process described here into the whole progress for the class.

ACT

1. Before going on, why not study the Romans 8 passage, using one or more of the guide questions and methods suggested, and develop your own summary statement or generalization of what the passage says? This should help you get a feel for your role in helping your teens develop principles from their Scripture study.

2. Study the passage of Scripture you'll be teaching in your lesson next week. If your lesson materials do not give suggestions for a discovery approach to the Bible study, see if you can develop your own. Build your plan around the four crucial teacher tasks in leading teens into personal study.

CHAPTER NINE
ENCOURAGING RESPONSE TO GOD

▶It's vital that your young people understand what the Bible teaches. Growth as Christians is intimately connected with knowing God's revealed will. But the teacher's task extends beyond communicating Biblical information. The real goal of Bible teaching is to lead learners beyond understanding—beyond a grasp of information—to faith response and obedience to what God's Word reveals.

We can never forget that the Bible is a personal Book, God's reaching out to us in love and guidance, and that His desire is for us to respond to Him personally too, to reach out, put our hand in His, and follow.

Nothing in teaching is as challenging or difficult as leading a class to respond to God. Here a teacher's skills and dynamic relationship with God blend together uniquely in the true fulfillment of his or her ministry. Here an understanding of the teaching-learning process and the power of one's own life with Christ are both demanded. And so in this chapter we'll look at three factors, combining skill and the teacher's impact as a person, that affect a teacher's effectiveness in leading youths to respond to the Word they have come to understand.

Guiding Exploration

In the last chapter we saw ways to lead teens to discover what the Bible teaches. And we saw that the teacher's final role in this part of the class process was to summarize the learning, to formulate a statement of the main truth (or truths) the passage teaches. At this point, moving into the LOOK and TOOK parts of the lesson, you are ready to relate what has been learned and stated to the purpose or transition statement with which you introduced the Bible study.

For example, in the last chapter, as one possible purpose statement leading into a study of Romans 8:18-30, the following question was asked: "Can life today really have purpose and meaning?" If you studied the passage and followed through on the *Act* assignment, you developed one or more summary statements on what the passage said concerning this issue. You may want to insert your own summary statements, but mine go something like these:

1. God has a purpose for all creation; it will be rescued from "the tyranny of change and decay."
2. God's Spirit in us works *now* to help us "in our infirmities."
3. Everything in our lives fits into His great purpose—to help us become more and more like Christ.

Having made these summary statements on the teaching of the passage, we want to go on to ask, "What practical impact can these truths make in my life? How can I respond to the things that trouble me, now that I know what God's purposes and ways of working are?"

There's usually a pattern that helps young people explore the implications of such truths for their lives and helps them define how faith might respond to God. For example, if in the HOOK discussion of the issue teens expressed concern about their own inadequacies or their inability to do or be what they want, you might guide them to explore the implications of God's present work in us in spite of our infirmities. You could ask, "Where do we feel inadequate? Where are we in trouble?" Their answers might include the following:

"When I pray."
"When I try to witness."
"At home. My sister and I argue a lot."
"It's hard to study for geometry."
"I don't read the Bible like I should."
"I don't really speak up when my friends do something wrong."

Your next step would be to have the teens discuss appropriate responses. You could ask, "What difference does the Holy Spirit make in these situations?" You might get answers like these:

"Maybe I could witness anyway—and trust the Holy Spirit to use even my mistakes."
"I could ask God to help me whenever I feel rebellious."
"Maybe the Holy Spirit can help me come across as myself and be accepted if I stand up against my friends when they're doing the wrong thing."

If in the opening discussion of the issue, the teens seemed more concerned about the tragic or disappointing experiences they and others face in life, you may focus on implications of my third summary statement—that God is working through every experience to shape us toward Christlikeness. You might ask, "What are some unexplainable things that happen to us?" Students might respond with answers like these:

"I flunked a test and got grounded."
"I was going with this guy, and he broke up with me."
"I can't get a job, and I really need one."
"Sue got sick and missed a whole year of school."
"My friend's cousin got AIDS through a blood transfusion. He's only four years old."

Responses could be sparked by a further question from you: "Can we see how God could use these?" Suggestions like these might result:

"I guess I could be more disciplined in the way I study."
"It's hard to know the reasons behind that."
"That was caused by the fact that there's sin in the world. But we need to show that we care when something like that happens. Jesus cared for people; so should we."
"We could learn to trust God anyway."

In both of these cases, your guidance is exerted to help teens state areas in which they or others feel inadequate or troubled. Then you encourage them to state how a knowledge of the Bible truth might help, or what kind of response to God in such situations is appropriate in view of what He has taught us.

When teens have suggested the response to God that is appropriate in the situations that concern them, when they have seen the differences that knowing this truth can make in their behavior and experience, then they will see the relevance of the Bible truth for their own lives.

Developing skill in guiding this kind of in-class exploration is important for effective teaching.

Modeling God's Truth

Understanding the practical implications of a Bible truth is crucial for response, but it is seldom enough. There needs to be a powerful motivation to respond.

It's at this point that we have to turn again to the importance of the Christian leader as an example, as someone who models the reality that the Bible invites the Christian to experience, as someone in whom the truth of what the Bible says can be seen incarnate.

Perhaps you've seen children standing hesitantly beside a lake after the first hard freeze, looking out at the ice but uncertain that it will hold them. Finally someone moves out, slowly, tentatively, and then with more confidence. The ice holds. Seeing the ice hold up their friend, the others find it easier to trust the ice themselves, and soon the whole group is laughing and excited as they slide and shout.

The Bible does something like this: It holds out the promise of a way of life that God says will hold up when put to the test. But it's hard to be the first one on the ice. It's easier to stand by the shore, wondering.

How important, then, to see a person who is older and more experienced stride confidently onto the ice, encouraging the others to come and join him or her. How important to have a living example, living proof, that God's Word is solid and real, and will hold up when put to the test.

This is one of the most challenging responsibilities of

the teacher. When we see ourselves as called by God to be examples, models, *leaders*, we can hardly come to class merely to repeat words we've read in some Sunday School quarterly, or to insist on the truth of a passage we've read in Scripture. We need to come to class having *experienced* the truth we'll explore with our teens, and with a willingness to share our experiences—both those in which we let Christ control and bring us victory, and those in which we turned from Him and failed. Then, sharing our *real* selves has a purpose far beyond the purpose we looked at in Chapters 5 and 7. Sharing is opening up our lives to others, that they might see the reality of Jesus Christ— both in the forgiveness He extends to us in our failures, and in the power He provides to enable us to overcome.

As you open yourself up to your students in sharing, you'll find that they respond by sharing themselves. By providing such an example, you'll begin development of an open, sharing atmosphere in the class. It is especially true in teaching teens: The teacher sets the tone. What happens when your students, following your lead, develop the freedom to share themselves and their experiences, too? They see the reality of Christ and the trustworthiness of His Word expressed by their peers as well. And, as young people are responsive to those their own age, even the most hesitant are likely to be encouraged to step out in faith.

Sharing, then, first by you and then by other young people, about how the Word you study together is experienced, is a basic and primary source of motivation to respond to God and *do* His Word.

Becoming Involved
One last element of motivation deserves mention.

Young people are motivated to respond when they see that someone *cares* about them and their lives in Christ, when someone reaches out to keep in touch during the week, when the teacher shows it is important to him or her that they go on with Christ, when they know someone stands with them in their problems.

The most successful teachers aren't those whose only contact with the kids is on Sunday morning. The most successful teachers are those who are available when kids want to talk. The most successful teachers are those who find time to drop around where kids hang out, and say hello. The most successful teachers are the ones who seek out the company of their students—inviting them to come along on an afternoon trip, to come over for a meal, to help in setting up chairs, to come to a basketball game. The most successful teachers are the ones who feel free to ask their students as friends, "How are things going? Have you been making progress with that problem you shared last Sunday?" The most successful teachers are those who can call to let a teen know, "I've been praying about that request of yours. How's it going?"

None of the things I've just mentioned should be seen as methods or gimmicks. All of them are simply indications of the quality of relationship that develops between a teacher and young people who become friends. And perhaps, after all, it's best to understand a teacher of young people *as* a friend who comes to know youths well and who is willing to show that he or she cares; who opens up his or her life to the teens, to show them both humanness and the transforming power of Christ who is at work within; who loves God's Word, seeks to grow closer to the One who speaks it, and is eager to lead those younger friends to know, love, and live the Word he or she has found so rich and meaningful; who guides—not with the authority of a distant "adult," but with the demonstrated authority of one who experiences what he or she teaches, and lives God's love; who, through word and example, gives teens the grow-ahead.

REACT

1. The LOOK and TOOK parts of the lesson structure are discussed in this chapter under the heading, "Guiding Exploration." Look over this section again, and then check back to see if you can see relationships between this part of the lesson and the HOOK. Particularly, how can a good HOOK discussion enrich the later search for varied applications?

2. This chapter has again suggested the importance of openness and self-revelation in your relationship with your students. How would you rate the atmosphere in your class now? Closed? Superficial? Opening up? Really open?

ACT

1. At the end of Chapter 1, I listed a number of questions that teachers of youth often ask. While I have not tried to answer these questions *directly*, I think you have seen in this book principles that point to answers for most of them.

    Go back now to those early pages, and see what answers you can give to each question. If you want to compare your answers with mine, you can look in the appendix which follows.

APPENDIX
QUESTIONS
ANSWERED

▶At the beginning of this book, I raised a number of questions about teaching teens. While these are not all answered directly in the book you've just read, I believe what has been said gives us a basis for answers. I think you'll find it most helpful if you go back to the questions now and jot down your own answers before going on to read mine. Comparison will, I think, be much more meaningful for you than simply looking over what I'll have to say.

With that suggestion given, here are my answers to the questions raised at the end of Chapter 1.

Teacher-Student Relationship
How is the teacher to relate to the teens he or she teaches? As a distant authority? No, this is just the stance teens most dislike and are most likely to reject.

As a friend before class, but firm guide and director in class? No, a teacher needs to be the same person in and out of the classroom. The secret of guiding learning is not in firmness but in knowing the structure of the classroom learning process and knowing how to gently direct the thinking of the group to that pattern.

As "one of the gang"? Of course not! The teacher is an adult, and the teens see him or her as an adult. He or she is a friend, but an adult friend.

What kind of relationship really facilitates Bible learning? An open, honest relationship in which members of the group are free to share their true thoughts and feelings and to tell their experiences. It is a relationship that breathes caring for one another.

How can that relationship be developed between teacher and class? In only one way: by the teacher setting the tone, providing the example. This involves the teacher treating young people with respect; it involves the teacher opening up his or her life to the teens in sharing; it involves the teacher experiencing the Word and demonstrating the work of Christ in his or her life. It involves being and becoming a friend to teens.

Teen Involvement
How much should teens be involved in the teaching-learning process, and what makes their participation meaningful? Fully! They are to be, and feel themselves to be, studying the Bible *with* you, not *under* you. Meaningful participation means that they study the Bible for help with problems they face or issues that are important to them, that they are responsibly involved in digging out the meaning of what a passage says, and that they discuss together in-depth implications of discovered Bible truths for their lives and daily experiences.

Are they to be listeners? Sometimes. But only sometimes. The passive role isn't one that leads to much learning.

Are they to think with the teacher about the meaning of the Biblical text? Yes, this is part of what they are to do. It's a first step, but there must be more.

Are they to share their lives and experiences? Yes, but not in a purposeless way. They are to expose their lives to the light of Scripture and see how they might respond to God's direction given there.

What kinds of participation make Bible study most meaningful? The kinds that let young people take responsibility. Looking up a verse and reading it is hardly responsible participation. Probing for meaning, for implications—this is really vital stuff, and the kind of involvement young people will see as significant.

How can a teacher get teens to participate on a meaningful level? By treating them with respect and all that we've seen that this means. By knowing lesson structure and guiding their thinking into the process pattern. Do these two things, and participation will develop. It may take some time. Many Sunday School teachers haven't taught this way, and so young people often don't know how to participate. But they can and will learn—more quickly than we think!

Teen Motivation

What makes teens want *to study the Bible?* Primarily awareness that what they are studying is relevant to them, and that God shows them a better way to live their lives.

Do we have to just "talk about whatever you want" to get interest? Of course not. It's helpful to know what teens talk about, surely. But the key to getting interest is to tie into something that really concerns them, and then show that God speaks to this issue.

What motivates young people, anyway? Life. They're real people, with real needs and concerns, with real relationships and situations that often trouble them. They know life is real for them and that their present experiences do count. Life isn't all "ahead" for teens. What they do and think and feel *now* makes a difference in their character and personality and their eternity.

How can we "tie into" their concerns and interests and lead them into the Bible? First we need to know our young people well. When we do know them, we can teach to meet their needs by showing them how God speaks about their concerns. The HOOK activity in the lesson structure is the first thing that happens in an effective class. And it does just this: it ties the study to follow into the teens' concerns and needs.

How can we motivate youth to do *the Word they hear?* By helping them see the implications of what they study for their own lives, by providing an example, and by personally showing an interest in them and their growth in Christ. It boils down to love.

Love them and show them by example that God's way is the best way for them. When teens are convinced that God speaks to them in love and that His way works—particularly when they see it in other teens as well as in you—their motivation to respond to God is high.

Content

We all agree that the Bible is the content we want to study. But what in the Bible do we want to focus on? We want to choose Bible content that gives God's guidance to teens in their present experience. This does not exclude doctrine. It simply means that we spell out the practical meaning of each doctrine we teach! For instance, I can't think of anything more practical for our decision making than the doctrine of

God's sovereignty. Because He is in charge of all, we are free to do the right thing in any situation.

How do we want to organize the content we teach? We want to organize it in such a way that the teens see the practical implications. The key to such organization is in the purpose sentence, or transition to the BOOK, discussed in Chapter 6. We want teens to come to Scripture looking for truth for life.

Do we just go verse by verse by verse? Not necessarily. We take a section of Scripture that deals with a developed thought, and we organize our lesson to understand that thought and then to spell out its implications for life.

How can we organize content effectively? Around a single, life-focused teaching aim that spells out a response to God that the passage we study indicates faith may make.

Purpose

What is the underlying purpose of our teaching? To lead our youths into a growing, responding relationship with God as His obedient children. To respond, youth have to hear God speak, and so must know the Word. But the goal of our teaching is to go beyond knowing, to doing. "If you hold to my teaching," Jesus said, "you are really my disciples. Then you will know the truth, and the truth will set you free" (Jn. 8:31, 32). The goal of teaching is to lead youths into discipleship, into doing God's Word, and discovering freedom in Christ.

Other Questions

What's the best way to use the short Sunday School hour? For older teens particularly, time is needed to work through the process. You may wish to eliminate the traditional opening and use the full allotted time for class. In fact, some churches have moved the "Sunday School" for teens to some weekday evening, where an hour and a half will be available for exploring Scripture and its impact on youths' lives in greater depth.

What's the best size for a junior high, senior high, or college-age class? Usually a junior high class runs well with six or eight kids. The number can be upped to a dozen for high schoolers—or even more—but here various methods should be used to break them down at times into smaller groups for direct Bible study and discussion. College-age classes are probably best when they run around a dozen also. Both high school and college classes can go higher—to 20 or even more. But here it's hard to keep the relationships in focus and give much individual attention. And we've seen how important that is.

How should we arrange the room? Try a circle from time to time, so the kids can see each other as they talk and share. Just switching from rows to the circular arrangement does a lot to change the atmosphere of the classroom and to open up participation. Let your room work for you. Arrange it in a way that best meets the aim you have set for each Sunday.

What's most important in teaching young people? You, the teacher. The person you are, the quality of your life with Christ, your openness and honesty, your skill in guiding the young people into deep exploration of God's Word—this is the key to giving teens the grow-ahead. It's great to realize, facing such a challenge and knowing our inadequacies, that Christ's Spirit is in us to help us in our infirmities! So trust Him, step out, and *teach!*